Writing about Theatre

WRITING ABOUT THEATRE

Christopher Thaiss
George Mason University

Rick Davis
George Mason University

Allyn and Bacon
Boston • London • Toronto • Sydney • Tokyo • Singapore

Vice President, Humanities: Joseph Opiela
Editorial Assistant: Rebecca Ritchey
Executive Marketing Manager: Lisa Kimball
Editorial–Production Administrator: Donna Simons
Editorial–Production Service: Matrix Productions Inc.
Composition and Prepress Buyer: Linda Cox
Manufacturing Buyer: Suzanne Lareau
Cover Administrator: Jenny Hart
Electronic Composition: Cabot Computer Services

Copyright © 1999 by Allyn and Bacon
A Viacom Company
160 Gould Street
Needham Heights, MA 02494

Internet: www.abacon.com

Between the time Website information is gathered and then published, it is not
unusual for some sites to have closed. Also, the transcription of URLs can result
in unintended typographical errors. The publisher would appreciate notification
where these occur so that they may be corrected in subsequent editions.

Library of Congress Cataloging-in-Publication Data

Thaiss, Christopher J.
    Writing about theatre / Christopher Thaiss, Rick Davis.
       p.   cm.
    Includes bibliographical references and index.
    ISBN 0-205-28000-5
    1. Dramatic criticism   2. Drama.   I. Davis, Rick.   II. Title.
PN1707.T45   1998
808.2—dc21   98-20080
                                                   CIP

Printed in the United States of America
10 9 8 7 6 5 4 3 2 1   03 02 01 00 99 98

CONTENTS

PREFACE

Writing about Theatre is the first text that directly addresses the writing needs of students in the theatre major and in literature courses that focus on study of the drama. Unlike the several existing texts devoted to "writing about literature" that include sections on "writing about drama," this text is the first that treats writing about the play—both as *text* and as *performance*—as a subject in its own right.

Moreover, by addressing both the student of theatre and the student of dramatic literature, this text shows how our understanding of drama is enriched by our critical attention to both performance and text. This volume will allow the teacher of literature, as well as the teacher of theatre, to assign not only the essential *critical analysis* of the play text but also *performance reviews, theatre history research,* and other projects that will enliven understanding and promote versatility.

For the theatre major, the book should be a consistently useful tool. In its sequence of chapters, it addresses projects of increasing sophistication, from those, such as performance reviews and play analyses, first assigned in lower-level courses to those, such as theatre history research and *dramatic theory* papers, assigned most often to advanced undergraduates. Those specializing in play production—directors, actors, designers, dramaturgs—should benefit from the blending in this volume of writing about aspects of production and analytical, historical, and theoretical writing about play texts. They will also find guidance on writing as a tool for developing production ideas.

For the student in the dramatic literature class, *Writing about Theatre* describes the two traditional genres of the *text analysis* and theatre history research. However, by adding attention to critical analysis of performance features, including acting, direction, and design, this book allows students to broaden their understanding of drama and deepen their insights into the dramatic text. In addition, the adjoining chapters on *dramatic criticism* (Chapter 4) and *text analysis* (Chapter 5) can give literature students practice in writing for different audiences, the play-going public and fellow literary scholars. Finally, Chapter 7, "Dramatic Theory and the Theatrical Essay," can show the more advanced student how to extend analysis from the single play to larger categories, e.g., a playwright's body of work or the functions of drama in a given society at a given time.

As a general guide to good writing, the text offers early chapters that show ways by which informal writing (e.g., purposeful note-taking, keeping of logs) promotes learning and critical/creative thought. A chapter on "writing as process" gives a four-step procedure that students and teachers can apply to any writing assignment, including those detailed in this volume. These *process* and *writing to learn* principles are reinforced in practical ways from chapter to chapter.

For the researcher, the book offers not only a step-by-step guide to the exploration of theatre history, but also an extensive bibliography of sources pertinent to each chapter and a guide to correct MLA citation of print and online sources.

ACKNOWLEDGMENTS

The ideas about the theatre that underlie this book are the result of a twenty-year conversation on which I have been a fortunate eavesdropper and sometime participant. Thanks, therefore, are due to some of the key conversationalists: at Lawrence University, Frederick Gaines, Richard France, Rachel France, and Mark Dintenfass; at the Yale School of Drama, Leon Katz, Richard Gilman, Stanley Kauffmann, and Michael Cadden; at the American Ibsen Theater, Michael Zelenak, Brian Johnston,Travis Preston, and the legions of dramaturgs; at Center Stage, Stan Wojewodski, Jr., Irene Lewis, and Peter Culman; at Washington College, Timothy Maloney, Jason Rubin, and the students who shaped my early efforts in teaching theatre and drama; and at George Mason University, my colleagues and students in the Institute of the Arts and across the campus, where the conversation continues growing livelier every day. To my co-author, Chris Thaiss, a peal of gratitude for involving me in his tireless advocacy of good writing, thereby sharpening my own commitment as writer and teacher. Thanks, always, to Julie for time, space, and support.

Rick Davis

Thanks to Joe Opiela of Allyn and Bacon for shaping my idea for a multidisciplinary writing text into a series of focused volumes, of which *Writing about Theatre* is one of the first two numbers. This project has brought me into collaboration with Rick Davis, my colleague on the Writing Across the Curriculum Committee at George Mason; for Rick's talent, energy, and graciousness I am most thankful. Brian Barker, poet and bibliographer, deserves thanks for the careful and creative research that produced our final chapter. Thanks also to the College of Arts and Sciences, Daniele Struppa, Dean, for supporting Brian's work on this project.

Of course, books such as this are not possible without the serious attention to writing given by faculty across disciplines in schools, colleges, and universities. My thanks go to the many members of the National Network of Writing Across the Curriculum Programs and especially to my fellow members of its board of consultants, including Pamela Childers, Toby Fulwiler, Bernadette Glaze, Richard Larson, Susan McLeod, Teresa Redd, Lex Runciman, Linda Shohet, Margot Soven, and Barbara Walvoord, who year in and year out provide leadership and inspiration. At George Mason University, the members of our WAC committee: Stanley Zoltek, Rick Davis, Ruth Fischer, Hun Lee, Eugene Norris, Mary Silva, Jeanne Sorrell, Ashley Williams, and Terry Zawacki, deserve my deep appreciation, as do the hundreds of colleagues in all fields who help to make our university a writing-rich environment.

At Allyn and Bacon, thanks also to Rebecca Ritchey and Lisa Kimball for their efforts toward the success of this project. For their constructive reviews of the work-in-progress, Rick and I thank Tom Adler, Purdue University; Jackson Bryer, University of Maryland; Richard Davis, Western Oregon State College; Ramon Delgado, Mountain State University; and Patti Gillespie, University of Maryland, College Park.

As always, no words can adequately express my thanks for Ann Louise, Christopher, Flannery, Jeff, Jimmy, and Irene, the perfect cast for our play, nor for Ann, whose direction is always inspired.

Christopher Thaiss

Writing about Theatre

1

DISTINCTIVE CHALLENGES IN WRITING ABOUT THEATRE

OUR SENSE OF THE READER

We intend this brief volume primarily for two types of reader:

- Those in undergraduate and graduate degree programs in theatre and drama
- Students enrolled in courses in literature that include dramatic works

As you will see throughout this text, we regard "writing about theatre" as encompassing many types of writing about the interdependent acts of *reading* plays, theatre history, and dramatic criticism and *seeing/hearing* play productions. We also include some material expressly for those involved in play *production*.

THE TWO MODES OF THE PLAY

In several ways the theatre challenges those who would write about it. First, it is an art form with two distinctly different modes of expression. **Theatre** usually refers to the performed play—a live encounter of actors and text with audience—while **drama** describes the playwright's work, the script, seen as a literary document. Both modes are proper subjects for the writer, but a clear sense of their differences as well as their interdependence is vital. Too often, writers about *theatre* ignore the values of the text, while writers about *drama* fail to recognize the special characteristics of performance. In this book, we will examine strategies for keeping both modes in mind in order to write vigorously and responsibly about theatre and drama.

Chapters 2 and 3 offer suggestions about the process of writing, from the development of an idea through the creation of the finished product. Helpful strategies for note taking; for writing to improve reading, listening, and observing; and for writing to experiment with style and voice are featured in Chapter 2, "Writing to Increase Learning." Chapter 3, "The Writing Process: Predrafting, Drafting, Revising, and Editing," focuses on the four processes that help the writer succeed in any form of writing about theatre. Chapter 8, "Sources for Writing about Theatre and How to Cite Them," provides a substantial list of print and online sources in the study of theatre as well as detailed information on how to cite sources.

Chapters 4 through 7 examine several principal types of writing about theatre and drama. The following is a preview of some of the issues we will consider.

CRITICISM AND REVIEWING: CAPTURING THE EVANESCENCE OF PERFORMANCE

A play unfolds on the stage. An actor gestures, an impact is made, and the moment is gone. A spoken line echoes and fades while the story is simultaneously told in the scenery and costumes and lighting and movement.

Any theatrical event of substance is a thing of many layers, sending complex signals to its audience in ever-changing configurations of meaning. A performance does not remain obediently open to a selected page, waiting for a coherent response to develop; it moves on, and so must the writer's perception. The writer must try to analyze in static words what has existed in sound and light and space and time.

Writing about performance, then, has much to do with *seeing* in an active and engaged fashion. To see well requires a process of imaginative re-creation as well as the ability to discern which of the many component parts of the theatrical event is responsible for the moment or the effect that we're trying to capture. When this work is done well, the critic can perform an invaluable function: highlighting the important and essential qualities of a performance that would otherwise be lost forever.

Critics, especially those working in the journalistic realm (newspapers, magazines, the electronic media), are also called upon to act as mediators between the art form and the audience. They help their readers understand and keep track of the latest developments in their area for a much wider audience than will ever see the events they write about. A successful play in a large, urban regional theatre might be seen by 30,000 patrons; the review of that play might reach a reading audience of close to a million. Just as a sportswriter writes the "game story" for those who didn't see the game, the drama critic writes, at least in part, for the benefit of those who cannot come to the show.

For some readers, of course, the review may become a key element in making the decision to see or not to see a particular production. While this is certainly a valid and time-honored function of arts criticism, it can tend to place the critic—especially those working in newspapers, radio, TV, and the Internet—in the role of "consumer reporter" and can lead to some uninspiring writing. After all, how much does the reader learn from a quickly decided verdict of "thumbs up"? And how definitive should the reader consider one critic's opinion to be?

In Chapter 4, "The Theatre Review and Dramatic Criticism," we will examine a method of constructing the play review so that both audiences are served: those who depend on the critic to keep them informed about the theatrical life of their times and those who are looking for guidance on where to spend their entertainment dollars tonight. We'll also illustrate how two critics seeing the same show might come to different conclusions about its merit based on their interpretive judgments about the play and the production.

PLAY ANALYSIS AND THE PERFORMING TEXT

Some writers might be tempted to abandon the slippery task of performance criticism, seeking solace in the quieter fields of dramatic literature. At least a playscript is available for consultation at leisure, and the reader controls the pace and the flow of the event. Marginal notes, dog-eared pages, and underlined passages belong to the ordered world of the study, not the headlong rush of impressions that we experience in the theatre, and play analysis has its comfortable analogues in the close reading of a poem, the explication of a novel. Surely this is the saner and more sensible way to work!

And yet the dramatic text has a way of asserting its theatrical rights. Good plays are not novels or poems disguised as dialogue; they are documents designed to provide a blueprint for the construction of the same rambunctious machine we were trying to escape when we fled the theatre for the quiet of the library.

The writer who chooses to work only with the printed page inevitably comes up against the text's sense of its own incompleteness, its hunger to be invested with all the bells and whistles, all the signals and noise that communicate so many of a play's meanings. Without quite knowing why it happens, the writer will be placed in the ironic position of creating his or her own theatre of the mind, doing the work that the text demands of its actors, directors, designers, and producers. Lines will start to come alive in this mental theatre; sets will be built, costumes sewn, music played, swords drawn.

In other words, to understand the totality of dramatic expression, the sensitive writer must be able to see and hear the theatrical explosions inherent in the seemingly quiet world of the text. *Good analysis of dramatic literature always takes the theatre into account,* and the statement works equally well in reverse.

In Chapter 5, "Text Analysis," we will examine two closely linked kinds of play analysis, *functional* and *literary,* and show how performance values can help unlock the power of the drama just as textual insights can form the basis for developing a sense of performance.

THEATRE HISTORY

Theatre and drama in some form have existed in virtually every culture throughout the world, with a documented history that goes back at least 2,500 years. Theatre has been a central form of creative expression and has served as the dominant form of popular culture. Sometimes theatre became a vehicle for social change.

The theatre's importance on the stage of world events, then, opens up a major field for scholarly inquiry: the history of the theatre—both as text and performance—and its relationship to larger societal currents. Here the challenge we face involves not only employing an engaged, creative sense of the theatrical event but also the ability to conduct skillful research in the history of the theatre and its sociopolitical context.

That context may be specific and local; there may be much to learn, for example, from a detailed research expedition into your own community's theatrical traditions. Or the context may be distant in time and broader in impact; what can we learn about the demise of Athenian democracy by reading the late plays of Euripides and Aristophanes next to the best historical scholarship of the period? Most investigations of theatre history inevitably lead the writer to some consideration of the surrounding society, and each kind of research tends to enrich the other.

In Chapter 6, "Theatre History," we will look at three kinds of theatre— the *physical theatre,* the *social theatre,* and the *performing theatre*—and suggest some ways to make the task of scholarship invigorating and original.

DRAMATIC THEORY AND THE THEATRICAL ESSAY

Almost any field of human endeavor can be very roughly divided into theory and practice, and the two sometimes don't seem to have much to do with each other. It is, after all, not strictly necessary to understand the theory of aerodynamic lift in order to fly an airplane, or the ins and outs of internal combustion to drive a car; you work the controls properly, and off you go.

In the theatre, there are those who concentrate on making plays and productions and those whose activity occurs at one remove. The latter group's job is to ask the underlying questions, such as: "Why do we make theatre?" "What constitutes a 'good' play or production?" "What is the value of drama?" "How do plays communicate meaning?" "What is the nature of representation?" For centuries, these and other questions were the province of philosophers and playwrights; since the Renaissance, however, dramatic theory has been developing its own set of practitioners. Today, a writer may choose to work in any number of contemporary theoretical modes, depending on individual beliefs and intellectual predispositions. Dramatic theory can become a battleground for issues that are also being fought out in the culture at large (e.g., feminism, multiculturalism, neoconservatism, etc.), and it can be an exciting forum for the exploration of new theatrical responses to a changing world.

The best dramatic theory, however, is written with one eye on the *practice* of theatre—as it is actually produced, and as it might be envisioned. Dramatic theorists know that for their work to have the widest possible impact, it must interact with the living art form, just as an aerodynamicist's drawings must be put to the test by an actual pilot in a real machine.

The *theatrical essay* is a variation on the theme of dramatic theory, offering a more personal view of a certain play, a writer's body of work, a distinguished production, a trend in the making. Different in tone and purpose from a review and less concerned with scholarly documentation than a research paper, the essay (sometimes referred to in journalistic circles as a "think piece") challenges the writer to stretch out a bit, to ruminate on a topic much in the manner of a columnist on a newspaper's op-ed page. In this kind of writing, the job is to make connections for the reader, to use the occasion of the subject matter to make a larger point, to provide a civilized meeting of the minds among author, subject, and reader.

Theatre and drama are rich fields for this kind of writing because they continually offer new examples, in the form of new plays and productions, upon which to draw. At its best, the theatrical essay can be a kind of thermometer with which to take the temperature of the times; even in less ambitious forms, however, the essay allows for a breadth of inquiry uncluttered by the scholarly apparatus of the historical research paper on one hand and unfettered by the narrow and specific purposes of the play review on the other.

Chapter 7, "Dramatic Theory and the Theatrical Essay," offers a way to begin thinking about the kinds of questions that dramatic theory and the theatrical essay can pose.

SUMMARY: THE FIVE MAJOR KINDS OF WRITING ABOUT THEATRE

This book examines the principles that underlie some of the main types of writing about theatre: the performance review, the text analysis (both functional and literary), the historical study, the dramatic theory essay, and the theatrical essay. We suggest procedures for developing ideas in each writing mode and offer possible formats.

The book is not intended as an exhaustive survey of the areas it describes—neither its length nor its purpose would allow that—but rather as a road map for the writer entering the subject of theatre and drama. The journey can be a fascinating one, since the play itself, in its two modes, offers such rich, diverse terrain for exploration and discovery. The skills practiced in creating the kinds of writing outlined here will serve to enhance your engagement with literature and performance of all kinds and to express that sense of engagement in clear and lively prose.

2

WRITING TECHNIQUES TO
INCREASE LEARNING

To live life fully is to live it as an act of criticism.
Writing is thinking and thought is language,
and to choose words is to imagine worlds.
—*BONNIE MARRANCA,* FROM HER SPEECH*
IN ACCEPTING THE GEORGE JEAN NATHAN
AWARD FOR DRAMATIC CRITICISM, 1985

While much of this book explains formal types of writing about theatre, this chapter focuses on writing tricks and tools that professionals in the field use informally to enhance their critical and creative thinking as well as recall of information.

A QUESTION OF ATTITUDE:
WRITING FOR YOURSELF

When your goal is to improve thinking and learning, it's basic that you experiment with writing in order to discover the techniques that work best for you. This chapter will describe a range of tools and approaches, but you should think of these as starting points only and should evolve personally successful variations. Keep in mind that the main—and often the only—reader of such writings will be the writer, so feel free to experiment.

---

*Published as "Acts of Criticism," in *Ecologies of Theater: Essays at the Century Turning* (Baltimore: Johns Hopkins University Press, 1996).

WRITING AND MEMORY: TAKING GOOD NOTES

For the specialized note-taking techniques of the **drama critic** during a performance, see the advice in Chapter 4 under The Practical Critic: A Few Hints.

In listening to lectures or discussions, people often regard note taking as a race. For fear of missing something, they try to scribble or type as fast as possible. Not only do they get fatigued quickly, but they also miss most of what they tried to hear.

Effective note taking should be carried out in at least two stages:

1. Quick **jottings** of key words or phrases during the course of a lecture or discussion.
2. **Summarizing** soon after the event, while memory is fresh and the jottings can spark fuller recall; the goal of this summarizing is to organize the information in some meaningful way, perhaps chronologically or according to greatest significance.
3. A third stage, **revision,** may follow if you are reporting the lecture or meeting to another reader in a report. Chapter 3 details ways to make your revising effective.

The writer should think of notes also as a basis for further dialogue with a speaker or discussants. It may be useful for the note taker to assume the role of the **investigative journalist,** who is not only interested in accurate recording and useful interpretation but also intends to follow up with questions about provocative, vague, or seemingly contradictory statements.

In this regard, the jottings you make during an event should reflect *both* your interest in capturing the **main concepts** of the event and your observation of what seems **puzzling** or **inconsistent** or **unclear.** Frequent use of the question mark in notes lets you keep track of concerns that demand follow-up dialogue.

Tools

Technically speaking, while paper and pen/pencil remain the technology of choice for most note takers, laptop computers are becoming more frequent. As long as they can be used comfortably and without keyboard noise distracting those speaking and listening, they provide the advantage of facilitating the revision of your summaries into essays for other readers.

Using Visual Aids, Prewritten Outlines, Agendas

Jotting occasional key words during an event allows you to attend to the visual dimension of a lecture, performance, or discussion, which may be just as meaningful as the heard portion. Body language and facial expressions may give at least as significant an indication of emphasis or doubt as does what is said, and you might reflect this information in notes, too.

If a lecture or panel includes any material via overheads or computer projectors, ask the speaker about access to those materials *after* the event. Since the visuals usually indicate a speaker's emphases, having outside access can save you much note-taking time and will guarantee greater accuracy.

The same goes for preprinted agendas or program outlines. These can guide note taking, since they indicate some of the speaker's emphases and how the speaker has organized the information. An outline sheet can be used as a kind of **template** for notes. You can elaborate on outline topics in the space available.

The Post-Event Summary

Writing up notes and your other observations soon after an event allows you to use short-term memory. The value of this exercise can't be overestimated, given the swift loss of most of these memories. Note taking during an event aids in retention but is no substitute for such a concentrated writing exercise as the post-event summary.

The most straightforward method of writing up notes merely elaborates on the **chronological flow** of an event. A typical lecture note:

> Tillyard—"Eliz. World Pict."—idea of ordered world—"great chain of being"
>
> in *T & C*—a Shak. "problem play"—Ulysses' speech

might become:

> Tillyard's *The Elizabethan World Picture* states that people in Shakespeare's time would have viewed the world as well ordered, with God at the head of a "great chain of being." Human society was thought to emulate this chain, with the King (or Queen) in the place of God and all other people in definite ranks down the hierarchy. Later critics have noted that it's ironic that one speech (by Ulysses) that Tillyard cites as clear evidence of this world view occurs in a play, Shakespeare's *Troilus and Cressida*, which ends with its society in chaos.

This kind of summary is no organized document, merely a fuller record of one's observations. Nevertheless, it can serve as a substantial basis for later study or adaptation into another document.

Alternatively, carefully reading over your jottings and thus "reliving" the event can give you a sense of a **center** or **focus** for your summary. Trying to find such a center is what the experienced news or sports reporter does after witnessing an event. This center is reflected in the reporter's **lead paragraph.** The rest of the details of the event are then ordered according to how they contribute to this central idea.

Be careful, however, not to jump to an impression of the event that isn't thoroughly substantiated by actual observation. *Read your notes thoroughly* before coming to an estimate of the central idea.

WRITING TO IMPROVE READING: MARGINALIA AND OTHER ANNOTATIONS

Writing in printed texts is a tried-and-true method for **remembering** and **thinking critically** about anything you read. If you are working on a book or xeroxed copy you own (and thus can mark up), always be ready with a pen or pencil to jot a comment or a question in the margins. Using this method of annotation is far superior to the popular method of applying yellow highlighter to any passages one thinks might be significant. *Writing* a comment or question gets the brain involved in thoughtful reading to a degree that mere highlighting can't approach. Besides, writing lets you express a wide variety of ideas and concerns about the text at hand; highlighting merely highlights. Sometimes readers unsure about which portions of a text might be more significant than others have highlighted whole paragraphs only to find out on rereading that the highlights have not aided retention and certainly provide them with no new information.

As with note taking on lectures and discussions, text annotation works best if you regard yourself as being **in dialogue** with the author of the book, article, or report. While certainly in most cases you can't easily make the comments and questions known to the author, writing those comments and questions forces you to **focus** and **articulate** your thoughts about an idea you've read. These annotations can therefore (1) serve as the basis of ideas that you can develop into a formal piece of writing, and (2) help yourself and others understand *why* you found the passage worth remembering.

Making Annotation Effective through Critical Questions

Skillful readers read with one or several purposes clearly in mind because definite purpose helps you concentrate on the reading. For example, the reader of a software manual reads better if he or she tries out the software immediately and needs answers to specific questions about installing and using the product. The skillful reader of fiction may want to compare features of an author's style to that of his favorite novelist. The clinical psychologist will read a case study more carefully if she has an eye toward understanding a patient with whom she is working. Even the student fulfilling a textbook reading assignment for a teacher can read with strong purpose, hence effectively, by applying well-known techniques.

If your specific purpose for the reading is not already clear, the most common way to give your reading purpose is to **ask specific questions** to guide your reading and annotation. Here are some examples:

1. *How would I summarize this reading for a person who has not read it?* The goal of this question is understanding of the **main concepts** in the work. As you read an essay on Tennessee Williams's *A Streetcar Named Desire*, for example, consider how you'd answer a fellow student's questions: "What is the essay about? What is its point? What is its main evidence?" Use the margins of the page or a separate sheet (or a computer file) to take notes toward building answers to these questions. For example, observe the annotations of the first page of an essay by Mary Ann Corrigan on this play. The annotations show the reader **paraphrasing** (i.e., using the writer's own words) and **summarizing** each paragraph, thus building toward a sense of the entire piece.

2. *In what ways does this work comment on issues or topics that are important to me?* If the work you are reading *seems* distant from your major interests, this question will productively test your imagination. Using this question, you watch for statements that bear on topics in which you do have some intellectual or emotional investment. Marginal annotations can track these connections. Writing can be especially valuable as a tool to forge connections where there don't appear to be any—and thus where you might have trouble feeling motivated to continue reading. For example, note this annotation by one reader of an essay on Aristotle's theory of tragedy:

> *Could this idea of "catharsis" help explain why so many people like terrifying films? Critics say that violent movies increase people's tolerance for actual violence and make them less sympathetic toward the victims, but Aristotle's theory maybe implies that a tragic* play *(including films) lets people express pity and fear in a controlled way, and so learn how to behave appropriately in a real crisis.*

3. *How can I simplify the language of this piece for someone who doesn't have a clue about the technical jargon?* Using this question as a guide will push the reader to get into and through the technical terminology to a better understanding of the concepts and details. Academic reading often remains opaque because readers don't make a concerted effort to penetrate the

On the morning after the premiere of *A Streetcar Named Desire* in 1947, Joseph Wood Krutch commented: "This may be the great American play." From the perspective of more than a quarter of a century later, *A Streetcar Named Desire* appears to be *one* of the great American plays. Its greatness lies in Tennessee Williams's matching of form to content. In order to gain sympathy for a character who is in the process of an emotional breakdown, Williams depicts the character from without and within; both the objectivity and the subjectivity of Blanche are presented to the audience. In *A Streetcar Named Desire*, Williams synthesizes depth characterization, typical of drama that strives to be an illusion of reality, with symbolic theatrics, which imply an acceptance of the stage as artifice. In short, realism and theatricalism, often viewed as stage-rivals, complement each other in this play. Throughout the 1940s Williams attempted to combine elements of theatricalist staging with verisimilitudinous plots and characters. His experiments either failed utterly, as in *Battle of Angels* in which neither literal nor symbolic action is convincing, or succeeded with modifications, for instance by the removal of the screen device in *The Glass Menagerie*. In *A Streetcar Named Desire* Williams is in control of his symbolic devices. They enable the audience not only to understand the emotional penumbra surrounding the events and characters, but also to view the world from the limited and distorted perspective of Blanche. The play's meaning is apparent only after Williams exposes through stage resources what transpires in the mind of Blanche.

Margin notes:

assessing *Streetcar*'s greatness

character shown both internally and externally

attempts at realism and theatricalism joined

Streetcar as first successful synthesis

stage devices as a window on Blanche

From Mary Ann Corrigan, "Realism and Theatricalism in *A Streetcar Named Desire*," in Harold Bloom, ed., *Modern Critical Interpretations of Tennessee Williams* (New York: Chelsea House, 1988), p. 49.

language. Readers often give up on difficult technical material, usually resigning themselves to their own inadequacy or to criticizing the author's style. Marginal writing forces the reader to slow down the pace of reading and strive to understand terms before moving on. For example, see how the annotation of the first page of an essay on "Dramaturgy as an Ecology" guides the reader's further work in the text.

In the twenty-five years since he first began a life in art, Robert Wilson has created an extraordinary number of works in theater, opera, video, furniture design, sculpture, painting, and drawing. Yet most of his theater productions of the last decade or more have rarely been seen in the United States, outside of New York, Boston, and more recently Houston. He spends the greater part of each year in Europe, producing works in the different media for its major theaters, opera houses, and museums. No contemporary theater artist's work travels from country to continent with such frequency or assurance.	diverse productivity!
	theatre work primarily European
	works on the move
The dislocation of contemporary artists and artifacts is duplicated in the lives of texts, increasingly at home on these transcontinental routes, dispersed from their own cultures. By that I mean the dispersed texts from lost civilizations, those of unknown or forgotten authors, the texts of books languishing on library shelves, exiled or censored texts, world classics. They are always at risk of becoming endangered species of writing. Time erodes their historical meaning; or, they can literally crumble and fall into pieces, like ruins. But there are those that find a home in today's world, preoccupied by preservation and travel. If the idea of the "dispersed" describes the lives of texts, Wilson's own manner of living and working in so many cultures and languages only stylizes the contemporary condition of relocation in literature. Today the natural state of writing is translation.	texts travel just like their creators
	"dispersal" in both place and time
	is Wilson's life itself a classic text in the making?
	pun on *translation,* "coming over to the other side. . . ."

From Bonnie Marranca, "Robert Wilson and the Idea of the Archive: Dramaturgy as an Ecology," in *Ecologies of the Theater* (Baltimore: Johns Hopkins University Press, 1996), p. 34.

WRITING TO IMPROVE READING: KEEPING THE READING RESPONSE LOG

While marginal annotation allows a reader to keep up a running critical dialogue with an author, the **reading response log** provides room for extended (or brief) reflection and analysis. Moreover, by its nature, this ongoing collection of **dated entries** allows you to observe changes in your perspective and growth in knowledge. Indeed, later entries that summarize and interpret this progress commonly characterize well-kept logs.

The reading response log is ideal for research. In writing play analysis, theatre history, and theatrical essays (see Chapters 5, 6, and 7, respectively), the reading response log can be an invaluable tool for annotating and critically summarizing any materials you read.

Tools

Though the word *log* usually sparks an image of a large hardbound ledger, more and more writers keep logs on computer. While the traditional book has the advantage of portability, the computer provides you ease in (1) **expanding** and **revising** a strong entry or series of entries into a formal article or report, and (2) **sending** an entry to a fellow reader via electronic mail.

Tips

Use the following tips for making your log more useful:

1. Always **date** entries, including the year. Even if the current entry adds to an earlier one, date the addition.
2. In referring to specific passages in a book or article, always take the time to **cite the work accurately.** Though log keepers usually want to avoid delays in getting their thoughts about a work onto the page or screen, making accurate citations eliminates the later frustration of being unable to locate important passages. (See Chapter 8 for rules on citation of sources.)

Techniques

Think of the log as being as flexible, experimental, or structured as you wish it to be. Because the log is a **personal document**—usually for the writer's eyes only—most log keepers appreciate the freedom it gives them to **explore** ideas and **experiment** with different styles and formats. On the other hand, the log also frees you, paradoxically, to impose on yourself the discipline of specific kinds of **critical analysis.**

Experimentation
On the side of experimentation, the log can be similar to the **commonplace book,** an age-old tool of scholars and writers for collecting and commenting on interesting text encountered in the course of study or casual reading. The **writer's notebook,** wherein professional writers try out imitations of style and collect impressions of events and people, is another experimental option for the log keeper.

Critical Analysis

On the side of greater analytic routine is the **scientific notebook,** that precise tool of the practicing scientist. In this form of the log, the scholar/writer observes and records phenomena according to strict methods of the discipline. Indeed, many scientific notebooks cross the line from the private to the public document because they can serve as legal documents in cases of patent or copyright dispute or in cases of alleged fraud or incompetence.

While we don't suggest that reading response logs should be taken so seriously in most instances, the log can be a good place to impose a regular analytic regimen on yourself. For example, one or more of the three basic analytic questions listed in the previous section can serve as a stimulus for writing about reading. To be more specific, let us say that you are doing research for a report on the comedies of Neil Simon and so are reading a series of reviews and essays on this playwright. In the log, you can apply question 1:

How would I summarize this reading for a person who has not read it?

to each source read, and this series of summaries might be easily adapted into the research report.

Similarly, you might also **create critical questions** to use as a regular framework for writing about reading. For example, it is common in scholarly research to question the credibility of an author; therefore, standard questions for the log might be:

What are the author's qualifications on this topic?

What are his or her experience and credentials?

What sources does he or she cite to substantiate any claims made?

What other evidence is presented?

Alternatively, a log keeper might want to make a **comparison** between and among the various sources a standard regimen for the log entries. For example, you might begin each entry as follows:

_____'s essay agrees and disagrees with _____'s position in the following ways.

As you accumulate sources and, therefore, comparative entries, you build an overall, integral sense of how all the sources contribute to understanding of the topic.

As emphasized earlier, in every case the questions you impose on your log should follow directly from your carefully thought-out purposes for reading.

WRITING TO IMPROVE OBSERVATION

Though every discipline relies on the student's ability to read critically, disciplines also demand the ability to observe and interpret other sense data. The sciences and social sciences obviously demand the researcher's keen attentiveness to sights, sounds, smells, and other phenomena. But the arts and humanities no less require a rich ability to perceive sensually and articulate those perceptions, as this talent is at the center of artistic creation and judgment. Writing can be a tool both to sharpen and to diversify our ability to perceive and understand sensual stimuli.

This chapter has described thus far three principal techniques for using writing as a tool of critical thought: note taking, annotating texts, and keeping a reading response log. The section on note taking mentions that notes should attend not only to what is said in lecture or discussion but also to **body language**—and, by extension, other observed phenomena, such as facial expression and tone of voice.

Both note taking and log keeping can be easily adapted to the needs of the observer of other phenomena. In this section of the chapter, we will suggest a few writing exercises that can make these tools especially effective.

Writing Dialogue: An Exercise in Listening

In this exercise, the writer's task is to record as closely as possible *exactly* what is spoken in a conversation and *how* the words are said. You might use a tape recorder and then transcribe the tape, but the important act in the exercise is to write as accurately as possible. In striving for exactness, you must pay attention to what you hear—rather than, as listeners usually do, trying to penetrate beyond or "inside" the words for what you either want or expect to hear. Such an exercise is valuable training for any number of disciplines, including medicine, law, law enforcement, nursing, social work, and psychology, where listening to clients or patients is a necessity. Theatre is an obvious example: The realistic reproduction of human speech is essential to the playwright, and the accurate hearing of dialogue is essential to the critic.

Close Description of Objects: An Exercise in Viewing

As with listening, seeing is often hindered by the human tendency to "correct" what is actually before one's eyes toward what one desires or expects to see. For example, one of the authors, to illustrate this tendency, routinely asks students early in a course to "draw a face." Almost without exception, the students look only at the empty page before them and draw their *idea* of what a face looks like. It is the rare student who in fact looks at another person's face and attempts to draw what he or she sees.

In this exercise, the writer contemplates two or more very similar objects—apples, for example. The writer then describes in as much detail as necessary one of the objects, so that *another person could identify* that *one object from all the others just on the basis of the description.* Not only does the writing force close examination of the objects, but it also challenges the writer to discover a range of **descriptive devices**—color, shape, statistical measurement, metaphor—to accomplish the fine distinctions.

Describing a Process: An Exercise in Narrative

Here the writer attempts to describe a brief process so that a person unfamiliar with the process can perform it. Such exercises, of course, are at the center of the scientific endeavor, since a basic purpose of the reporting of experiments is to enable other researchers to perform the same experiment. But **process description** is equally central to teaching the methods of every discipline; moreover, business success and effective government depend on the ability to communicate clearly **instructions** for everything from filling out tax forms to taking pain remedies to working a video camera.

Practicing process descriptions frequently teaches a writer:

1. *Respect for different readers:* How technical can my language be? How can I inform the novice without sounding condescending to the more knowledgeable?
2. *Close attention to even the smallest step in a process:* Testing process descriptions usually reveals that the writer has overlooked small steps that are performed unconsciously.
3. *Diverse ways to "bring alive" a narrative:* Writers learn to give vivid examples, create interesting characters, and use graphics and metaphors.
4. *Respect for feedback and revision (the "process" of writing):* The test stage of a process description almost always teaches a writer that revision is essential for any piece of writing to meet a reader's needs. (See Chapter 3 for details on learning and applying these stages of the writing process.)

"How to Build a Flat" is a sample process description from theatrical design. Observe how the writer has limited the use of technical language and used some of the devices noted in item 3.

WRITING TO EXPERIMENT WITH STYLE AND FORMAT

A great way to learn from writing and to have fun while learning is to **experiment:** to play with language, point of view, the appearance of the

---

Sample Process Description
"How to Build a Flat"

Definitions

flat: a standard piece of theatrical scenery, usually consisting of a lumber frame and a covering of either painted canvas or a hard surface such as plywood or luan.

toggle brace: horizontal member, usually running across the middle of the flat. Helps the flat retain its shape.

corner brace: diagonal members, usually running from one of the outside verticals to the top and bottom rails, for stiffness.

corner block: a 1/4" plywood triangular block or plate that joins a vertical to a horizontal member of the flat, with glue and nails.

keystone block: a 1/4" plywood keystone-shaped (or rectangular) block or plate that joins a toggle brace to the main verticals of the flat.

framing square: an L-shaped tool used to establish a perfect 90° angle.

Process

1. Determine the required size and shape of the flat, whether any openings (e.g., for a door or a window) are needed, and the materials from which the flat is to be built.
2. Draft a working drawing of the flat, showing exterior dimensions, all interior braces (such as a toggle and corner braces), and all fasteners (such as corner blocks and keystone blocks).
3. Make a "cut list" of all the pieces of lumber showing their proper lengths. Be sure to take into account which pieces will sit inside the verticals and which will run the full width of the flat; and remember that verticals sit inside the top and bottom horizontal rails.
4. Cut the lumber to the sizes on the cut list.
5. Using a framing square, assemble the outside frame of the flat. Join each corner with a corner block, glue, and nails. Be sure that the grain of the plywood corner block runs *across* the joint (for rigidity and strength). Also be sure to *inset* the corner blocks 3/4" from the top and sides of the flat to allow for joining other flats at a later time.
6. Lay in and join the toggle brace and the corner braces to the flat frame, using keystone blocks, glue, and nails.
7. Turn the flat frame over, cover, and paint as desired.

---

document, and the many other variables that go into writing. Up to this point, this chapter has emphasized using a log as a way to practice over and over certain critical questions as a way to make reading and other observations more meaningful. Here we suggest that an equally important function of writing, whether in a log or in separate exercises, is to do things differently from writing to writing.

While later chapters will present some standard formats for documents in theatre, keep in mind that the potential for writing in any discipline extends far beyond the standard or customary. Indeed, writers can't bring ideas to some readers without trying out designs, "voices," metaphors, and other elements that might strike some as strange or even wholly new. For example, just a few years ago the idea of composing business "documents" with sound and video would have seemed like science fiction. But now, thanks to the enterprise and imagination of a few, Internet-based business is a booming industry.

Writers have always had at their disposal a wide variety of options in style—essays, stories, poetry, song, and drama are a few of the better-known ones. Now, however, with widespread access to sophisticated graphic and presentation software, the average writer has choices that formerly belonged only to a handful of skilled artists and craftspeople. For example, the writer who, regardless of formal training in art, works in the medium of the Internet not only can manipulate the printer's palette of font, sizes, color, and arrangement, but also can adapt the most sophisticated graphic—even cinematic—effects by importing material from other sites on the Net. A writer who creates an electronic folder of stylistic experiments is, in truth, creating an electronic log that teaches in the doing and that can be used as a sourcebank for other projects.

Even without employing computer technology, writers in any discipline can productively and enjoyably experiment with style and design. An excellent way to get started is to imagine how your language, layout, information, or tone of voice would have to change if a **radical shift in audience and purpose** of the document should occur. For example, see the excerpt from a well-known critical review by Robert Benchley, who wrote this essay for *The New Yorker* in 1936; as you read, think about the writer's purposes in the document and about the characteristics of the typical reader. (You might try annotating the text toward understanding purpose and audience.)

Now imagine a dramatic shift in audience and purpose: this review has been reimagined as a set of notes from the director to the company, with the purpose of inspiring an even better performance the next night; or an imaginary conversation between two actors mentioned prominently in the review, with the purpose of poking ironic fun at actors' "friendships."

In experimenting with changes in style and format, consider some of the following categories:

- *Level of technical language:* What words need to be defined? For which terms should substitutions be made? Should some ideas be eliminated altogether or spoken about only in metaphor?
- *Tone:* Play with mood: threatening, carefree, cryptic, earnest, fanciful, professional/technical, reassuring, etc.
- *Syntax:* Short, simple sentences? Long, complex ones? Questions?

John Gielgud's Hamlet comes to us from London, where it has had an enormous success. This seems only logical, for it is a Hamlet that you will remember—intelligent, sensitive, and at times inspired to the point of lifting your orchestra chair a few inches off the floor with you in it. It is in its sensitive intelligence, I think, that it excels.

As so often happens, a highly sensitive intelligence sometimes swings around into a neurosis, and there were times when I felt that Mr. Gielgud was letting himself go at the expense of the lines he was reading, but these moments were few and far between. And to complain of Hamlet's being neurotic is, I suppose, like complaining of Ophelia's being mad or Polonius's being verbose. Hamlet's nerves could not have been what you would call "in the pink." I will take gladly the few jumpy moments that Mr. Gielgud gave me and discount them for the many more moments of genuine excitement.

In case my vote is needed, however, to settle a tie between John Barrymore and John Gielgud, I must admit that for my money (a pass) Mr. Barrymore's Hamlet was more to my liking. There was a humor there . . . which happened to fit in with my own personal feeling about Hamlet. . . . Mr. Gielgud smiles, it is true, and smiles at the right times, but it is a sad smile, a smile of infinite sweetness, and bodes no ill to anyone. Mr. Barrymore's smile was the smile of an actor who hates actors, and who knows that he is going to kill two or three before the play is over. I am not an actor-killer, but I like my Hamlets to dislike actors, if you know what I mean, and I think you don't. . . .

There was a feeling, however, in my own mind that things were not going well in Denmark. I was afraid for the success of the whole evening, and I was frankly glad when it was over. For the first time, I was definitely not excited by Mr. Mielziner's settings, which in one particular instance reminded me of a dining room in the Bronx.

- *Person and voice:* Personal and active ("I'd do X and so should you")? Impersonal and passive ("Research was conducted that might suggest . . . ")? Consider how person and voice can affect the reader's respect for your position and interest in what you have to say.
- *Use of story and character:* "Imagine walking into a big room that smelled like . . . "; "Von Delbach stumbled on this technique when she was working on. . . ." Story and character usually increase a reader's attentiveness.
- *Formatting:* Conventional paragraphing versus much indenting, use of "bullets," boldface type, shifts in font, size, and other features.

Here are two stylistic experiments based on the Benchley review:

Experiment 1: A Set of Notes from the Director to the Company

Great job last night, everyone. We can look forward to a terrific production. Here are just a few things to work on for tomorrow's rehearsal:

- John: in the "To be or not to be" soliloquy, I felt that you were going too far in the direction of self-pity (this also happened in the "O what a rogue and peasant slave am I" speech, but for different reasons). Let's try the idea that Hamlet is using this speech to *explore* the ramifications of suicide, not so much that he's actually on the brink of it.
- John (and this note is also for Rosencrantz and Guildenstern): we need to see more of a sense that Hamlet is getting desperate enough to be *dangerous* to the Court. His glee at feigning madness might be masking something real. You're giving us the madness but without the glee. It's the twinkle in his eye and his smile that makes us really worry about him: In other words, danger not pathos. Work on that smile.
- Designers: can you do something to make Gertrude's bedroom scene look a little less domestic? Think more medieval and less contemporary—maybe the weight of the drapery is wrong? Also it could be just a little darker; this is a world lit with torches, after all.
- All: keep the energy and the concentration up right through to the end. The play should keep gathering momentum right up until Hamlet dies, and then it's almost over. Right now we seem to be losing steam by the time Hamlet leaves for England. Place yourselves in the situation of people who have an enormous communal problem to solve, on which hangs not only their own lives but the fate of their country. Every single character has a great investment in that solution.

Experiment 2: An Imaginary Conversation between John Barrymore and John Gielgud (two of the greatest actors of the twentieth century)

(Scene: A heavenly version of an actor's after-theatre club: dimly lit, with heavy leather chairs and dark wood-paneled walls. John Barrymore is having a drink and perusing a well-worn copy of Hamlet *when John Gielgud walks in.)*

Barrymore: Well, John. Good to see you here at last. Sorry about that Hamlet review. I saw you, and I thought you were terrific.

Gielgud: Did you really? Why didn't you come backstage after the performance? I could have used some expert cheering up.

Barrymore: Oh, I'm never comfortable doing that. Besides, I didn't like the Gertrude and I would have had to make up some transparent lie on the spot. "Oh, Judith, now that was *quite* a performance" or something like that. They always know.

Gielgud: It's like old Benchley said in that notice: You had the smile of an actor who hates actors. I happen to like them.

Barrymore: Well, so do I, man. He was talking about Hamlet, not me. By the way, I rather agreed with him there.

Gielgud: What do you mean? What did *he* mean, for that matter?

Barrymore: In a nutshell—

Gielgud: And where in the devil is that waiter?

Barrymore: Oh, the service takes years here. In a nutshell, then— Hamlet's a bit of an actor himself, would you agree?

Gielgud: Of course, but not by choice. He's forced into it.

Barrymore: We may disagree there, but no matter. He "puts an antic disposition on" to shake things up a bit around Elsinore. It gives him a kind of license to be bad that his melancholy attitude didn't.

Gielgud: Are you saying he doesn't really go mad?

Barrymore: I'm saying he *starts* to go mad and then devises a way to contain it by playacting it. That's where my smile came in—my Hamlet was enjoying the game. Yours was feeling a little too sorry for himself. My Hamlet scared the Court a little—yours made them sad. It's all in the smile, my dear boy.

Gielgud: Is everyone in this club going to talk to me like a critic? And where the devil is that waiter?

GOING PUBLIC: FROM WRITING FOR YOURSELF TO WRITING FOR OTHERS

The next chapter will describe techniques for transforming the writings you do for yourself into documents you intend for others. Going public with writing has often stopped would-be writers, who fear the scorn of readers. Keep in mind, however, that if you regularly practice using the tools and techniques described to this point, your confidence will increase as your skills grow and diversify. With practice, tools such as the log and a ready bank of questions for critical reading, seeing, and listening, there is no reason why a writer should ever be stymied by a blank page or screen.

3

THE WRITING PROCESS: PREDRAFTING, DRAFTING, REVISING, EDITING

GENERAL PRINCIPLES BUT NO SINGLE FORMULA

In its details, the writing process varies for every person. Even for the same writer, the process will vary somewhat from task to task. When composition specialists talk about the **writing process,** they mean several things: for example, the steps and the attitudes through which a writer proceeds toward completing a writing task, whether it be a memo to a co-worker, a research report to a professor, or a letter to a relative. Understanding how writers accomplish such tasks helps composition researchers improve the teaching of writing and the development of teaching materials.

To the composition scholar, the writing process also means a general progression that is exemplified over and over in the work of experienced writers, regardless of the field. Though different scholars have given differing names to these stages of the writing process, they are most commonly referred to as *"prewriting"* (in quotes because we will be substituting what we feel is a more appropriate term), *drafting, revision,* and *editing.* Each stage will be examined in this chapter. Chapters 4 through 7, which describe common tasks and formats in writing about theatre, follow from the principles of drafting and revision described here.

PREDRAFTING AND DATA COLLECTION

Like anything else worth doing well, writing requires **planning** and investing a good bit of time *before* you sit down to create what will become the finished work. In the case of writing, this means that you should plan to do some, often considerable, writing before you actually draft the review, analysis, history, or essay.

Chapter 2 describes such writing tools as the log, which can be very valuable in this planning phase. Depending on how it is structured by the writer, the log can help you:

1. Plan the **content** and **organization** of any written work.
2. Sort through and **evaluate** readings and other data you plan to use.

As described in Chapter 2, the log can also be a place where you **experiment with style and format** for the project being launched.

The work you do before drafting is often referred to—somewhat misleadingly—as "prewriting." A more appropriate term would be **predrafting,** since, as we've seen, much writing is often involved in the planning stage of any project. Indeed, if you use this planning—predrafting—stage for log keeping, as described in Chapter 2, some of what you write experimentally in the log may indeed find its way into the actual draft.

The keys to successful predrafting are **patience** and an **open mind.** The more complex a writing task, especially the less knowledgeable you are about the subject and format of the project, the higher percentage of the total project time you will need for predraft work. You should not be surprised to find that 80 percent or more of total time spent on a project will be devoted to the predrafting stage of, say, a piece of original research. Writing during this stage, perhaps kept in a log (as noted in Chapter 2), might include:

- **Notes** on lectures, interviews, conferences, or experimental procedures
- **Annotations** in books and on articles
- **Summaries** of notes and annotations
- **Experiments** in style and format (see Chapter 2 for more detail on these techniques)

Patience is vital in allowing this rich process of reading, talk, procedure, and analysis to shape the ideas that will be central to the draft.

An open mind is similarly essential. The purposes of the predrafting stage are **learning** and **critical thinking.** Writers who, because of haste or impatience, move too quickly to the drafting stage, jump to opinions about data and then feel constrained *by the draft* from collecting more evidence and from doing fresh thinking. **Budgeting** sufficient predraft time and **using critical thinking** tools such as the log almost always ensure a better finished product, but you need to be patient and willing to learn in order to be comfortable with these aids to writing.

Doing a Dummy Draft

One experimental technique that can be part of the predrafting stage is what we call a **dummy draft:** not really a draft that incorporates all of your note taking and summarizing but an attempt during your predrafting to *set down in an organized way what you have learned about the subject so far.* This dummy draft can be part of the log. Its purposes are:

1. To **bring together** the many **details** you have accumulated during predraft research in order to let you see what has been accomplished to this point.
2. To show you **gaps, flaws, and inconsistencies** in the research, and thus indicate what still needs to be done.

Like the dummy models that engineers create during a design process, this draft lets you *test out* ideas and wording. The dummy draft is informal, its only reader is the writer (and perhaps a close colleague who has agreed to give feedback on the preliminary work). This piece can help satisfy your anxiety about the sufficiency and significance of the research to this point. It can also be **concise,** just long enough to achieve the two purposes noted above.

To show something of the flavor of such a work, here is an excerpt of a dummy draft by one of the coauthors about his research for an article on George and Ira Gershwin's *Of Thee I Sing.* (The final draft of this article appeared in *American Theatre* magazine in 1992.)

> The country lies mired [wallows?] in a painful economic downturn. One party has held a twelve-year lock on the White House. The fall election campaign is stuttering forward in search of a defining issue. [how long can I maintain the political parallel without mentioning the show?]
>
> Strenously avoiding anything resembling a position, one of the candidates sweeps to victory on the Love platform, marrying a wholesome girl and winning over the voters by showing them the very model of a modern American couple.
>
> Suddenly a scandal erupts involving a broken promise to a beauty queen by the new President—rotten timing, too, because the First Lady has just struck a blow for family values by delivering twins. Disgrace is held at bay [how about—An international incident is averted? The first is more immediate, the second is closer to the plot] when the heretofore ineffectual Vice President marries the beauty queen, and the Union is saved.
>
> This tabloid account of a misbegotten political season [the TV movie cliché "ripped from today's headlines!" comes to mind here]

explains why that landmark American musical, *Of Thee I Sing*, is once again sweeping the country. [How much production history do I need here? Any? Try focusing on just the opening of the show and its current revivals] The 1931 collaboration of George S. Kaufman and Morrie Ryskind (book), and George and Ira Gershwin (music and lyrics), opened on the day after Christmas in a year that found Americans' confidence in their elected government at an unprecedented low. It seems eerily prescient [maybe all too contemporary?] this year. No wonder four regional theatre companies have scheduled campaign-season productions: Washington's Arena Stage, Pennsylvania's Bloomsburg Theatre Ensemble, the Cleveland Play House, and Chicago's Remains Theater. [next two paragraphs—recap plot, stressing parallels to today's politics—Look at director interviews to see if they mention anything that needs preparation in the plot summary—then from there move into discussion of each new production—stress contrasts—somewhere near end find place for Juvenal quotation about how it's difficult not to write satire.]

Predrafting and Specific Writing Tasks

The following chapters will briefly describe appropriate predraft writing for such specific writing tasks in theatre as the play review, play analysis, theatre history, and theatrical essay.

DRAFTING: A CHANGE IN ATTITUDE

Moving from the predraft to the drafting stage involves a change in attitude. The most useful attitude to take toward the varied writing in the predraft stage is **experimental;** the main audience is you, the writer, and the primary purpose is **learning.** When you **draft** in earnest, the most useful attitude is still experimental, since you must feel that whatever is being written is only being **tested out** and can be revised. However, the sense of audience has changed: now you are directly attempting to reach other people with definable characteristics as readers and definable needs for information. The basic purpose has changed, too, from your own need to make sense of reading and other phenomena to **meeting the needs of those defined readers.**

These changes mean that the drafting writer writes with a double consciousness: with an **open mind**—that is, with an eye toward possible revision—and with a **sense of limits** imposed by the purposes and the possible readers. Thus, the drafting writer has a very focused intent: "I'm writing this the way I want it to look to my intended reader"; yet the writer feels the ease of knowing that *this is not a final draft* and hence can ask for

feedback—critical commentary—on this draft that can lead to productive revision.

How Rough Is the Rough Draft?

Unlike the dummy draft described under Predrafting, a so-called **rough draft** should be intended to *stand as a final product,* unless feedback dictates that revisions are needed. In either academic or workplace situations, when teachers or supervisors ask to "see a draft," they almost always mean a seriously written effort that incorporates the writer's best thinking and most thoughtfully analyzed evidence. A rough draft is like a rough diamond: not polished, but still a diamond.

That's why the so-called "rough" draft comes *after* the intensive work of predraft writing and research. Inexperienced writers often make the mistake of putting off the hard work until after the rough draft, which itself appears shoddy and which comes too late in the process to allow for the careful study and critical thinking that should have occurred predraft.

PLANNING THE DRAFT: THE THREE KEYS

During the predraft stage, writers should of course be guided in their research by their **thoughtful understanding** of the **purposes** of the project. As illustrated in Chapter 2, the writer who has a clear sense of purpose will learn the most and think most productively about any subject.

Also useful in the predraft stage, but absolutely essential toward writing a solid draft, will be clear understanding of two other factors: **format** and **audience.** With purpose, these are the three keys of good draft writing.

Formatting the Draft

The **format** comprises both the **organizational structure** and the **appearance traits** of the draft. Chapters 4 through 7 will describe several typical formats of writing in theatre. Nevertheless, be aware that it is hard to generalize about format, because the "right format" for any given document will probably include:

1. Highly specific requirements in the particular situation
2. Leeway for the writer's creativity

Learning the Highly Specific Format Requirements
If you are responding to an assignment from a particular reader—say, a professor, work supervisor, client, or grant committee—**assume** that there are specific format requirements and **seek** to learn them. Don't be misled by

the assigner's silence about format; he or she may be assuming that you already know all the tiny rules *or* the assigner may have never given thought to what he or she expects—such readers often say things like, "I'll know what I want when I see it."

There are two basic ways to seek the specific formatting:

1. Ask (see the checklist of typical formal characteristics).

2. Study and emulate earlier documents for the same purpose and the same reader. For example, grant agencies usually make available on request successful previous applications. Businesses keep files of their documents, which can be used by new employees as models of style and format; professors often do as well.

   Caution: When you review files, be sure to check with a knowledgeable person, such as the person assigning you the task, about *which* documents might serve as models. Particularly in the workplace, files are as likely to contain bad models as good. Ask your reader to review a potential model before you base your own writing on it.

When you are **asking** about format, the following checklist of **typical format characteristics** may be helpful:

- *Correct spelling, punctuation, and Standard Edited American English (SEAE) syntax:* Assume these are required unless otherwise informed.
- *Order of information:* Should the draft be organized in sections? If so, in what order?
- *Use of headings and subheads:* Should sections of the draft have headings (titles)? What headings should be used?
- *Margins, spacing between lines, and indentations:* Are there specific rules for these?
- *Boldface type, italics, underlining:* What sorts of items should receive these kinds of emphasis?
- *Number of words or pages, minimum and maximum*
- *Type style (font) and size*
- *Illustrations, photos, charts, and graphs:* Are these required? Frowned on? Are there size and style restrictions?
- *"Special effects"—video/audio:* Can video- or audiotapes accompany a written draft? How fancy should a web page be? If these effects are used as addenda, how should they be referred to in the written text?
- *Cover pages or cover letters:* Should these be used? If so, what information should they contain, in what order, and with what appearance?
- *Footnotes, endnotes, and citations:* Is a specific documentation style favored? (See Chapter 8 for more on this part of formatting in writing about theatre.)

- *Appendices and other addenda:* Are these allowed or encouraged? If so, are there page limits? How should data in the appendices be cited in the main text?
- *Quality of paper or other materials*

If you are **following earlier models** in formatting the new document, the checklist of typical format characteristics may also be helpful in analyzing the models. Do not hesitate to ask the intended reader questions about formatting, audience, or purpose that may arise in reading the model documents. For example, it's common for model documents to provoke questions about **formality** or **informality of tone,** about the **technical level of the language,** and about the **level of knowledge assumed in the reader.**

Two General Rules of Formatting

In the absence of specific information from a reader or of sample documents to use as guides, two all-purpose formatting rules of thumb can be used:

1. *Be simple and consistent:* Most readers respond well to clear layouts and consistent use of spacing, indentation, and other features; frequent shifts in font and type size tend to distract and confuse.
2. *Format so that readers can grasp your main ideas as quickly as possible:* Judicious use of headings, spacing, indentation, and emphasis (boldface, italics) guide the reader's eye as the writer wishes. Long paragraphs, tiny type, and little white space tend to confuse and bore.

Drafting for Your Audience

Unless you write only for yourself, you write for more than one audience: yourself and at least one other person. Even the audience of the self changes depending on mood, fatigue, and your latest experience. So drafting for your audience is no easy task, and it becomes more difficult the more readers who are involved.

Of course, the more practice you get writing for certain readers, the more you can assume and the easier the task becomes. But whenever the writer, no matter how experienced, tries to reach a new reader, some planning is called for.

As with learning about format, learning about other traits of audiences may require **asking readers** and **using model documents.**

Talking with Readers (and Writers)

Don't hesitate to request further information about new assignments from teachers or supervisors. Some common concerns are those noted earlier:

- **Tone:** How businesslike? Reserved? "Official"? Impersonal? Friendly? Solicitous? Glib?
- **Level of technical language:** Which terms should be defined? Should any terms be avoided?
- **Assumed knowledge of topic or issue:** Should I assume that the reader has also read the critics? Has the reader already seen the play? Does the reader already have a particular viewpoint on this controversy?

By all means, be sure to ask readers if they are willing to give feedback on a draft of the project. Receiving such an invitation may be a writer's best means of ensuring a high-quality final draft. (See "Feedback" in the Revision section of this chapter.)

Also don't hesitate to talk with **writers more experienced** in performing the kind of task you've been given. Even the simple question "What should I look out for?" will usually provoke an informative response.

Learning from Previous Models
Besides using the checklist of typical format characteristics, apply to previous examples the questions about tone, level of technical language, and assumed knowledge under Talking with Readers.

An Audience Exercise for the Log
Before drafting, write an audience analysis as part of your log. Use this writing to think about characteristics of the various groups who might read your work. Make some preliminary decisions about tone, technical language, and assumed knowledge.

Knowing the Purpose(s) of Your Draft

The third key to good drafting is being sure of your purpose. As with format and audience, **asking readers and experienced writers** and **learning from previous models** can provide insight about your purpose. (See the previous sections on Format and Audience for details.)

Be aware that the purposes of any document are multiple. Even a two-line scribbled memo to a co-worker, "Let's talk at lunch about the changes in the set design," can have many intents, most of which may be indirect: (1) "Let's talk at lunch about the changes in the set design"; (2) "I'm including you and excluding _____ from our talk"; (3) "I'd like to have lunch with you"; (4) "I hope you'll have lunch with me"; (5) "This is hand-written and off the cuff; it's no big deal if you refuse"; and so on.

When talking to a reader or a more experienced writer, show awareness of these multiple purposes: instead of asking, "What is the purpose of this document?" ask "What is the most important purpose? If it does nothing else, what must it accomplish? What are some other purposes it should achieve?"

A Purposes Analysis Exercise for the Log

Before drafting the project, use this log piece to help you list and prioritize the purposes of your project. It may help you discover purposes of which you had not been aware; it may help you decide which information should come first (that is, in the position of greatest importance in most academic and business documents).

EFFECTIVE REVISION

While any experienced writer would agree that "writing is rewriting," making that rewriting, or **revision**, effective calls for sound strategies, not just good intentions.

First, let's clarify what we mean by revision. Basically, composition scholars define revision as

1. Changes that a writer makes to a draft *while* it is being written; as writers compose, they return to earlier portions of a draft and change the text in response to fresh insights.
2. A more **systematic process** by which a writer submits a draft to a reader or readers for **feedback** and then makes changes based on reader commentary.

Revision is *not* to be confused with the copyediting, proofreading, or re-copying that writers do before submitting a final draft to a professor, boss, client, or other reader. Such changes don't involve the thoughtful, often imaginative "re-seeing" that characterizes revision.

Why Do Writers Revise?

As part of the normal process of communication, more than one draft of a spoken or written statement is often needed in order for a message to be clearly understood. Inexperienced writers often wonder why writing over which they have exercised great care still fails to communicate. Experienced writers have learned that the need for revision is normal, not usually a sign of either the writer's or the reader's incompetence.

Moreover, experienced writers have also learned to use revision as a way to intensify and expand their own thinking. Trying out different phrasings, different organizational patterns, and different ideas changes your perspective on any task or topic. Using revision in this creative way often leads to a far better product.

Techniques for Effective Revision

Using Wait Time

Always try to budget some **wait time** into the writing process. The more time away from a draft you are working on or one that you have completed the better able you will be to *see the work as another reader might see it.* In the midst of composition, your mind will be so full of the ideas that you want to convey that it will be difficult for you to detect gaps in reasoning or unclear phrasing.

Even overnight may be enough time for you to clear your mind sufficiently to allow for what is called **distancing** from a draft: that ability to see as others might see the writing. Wait time is especially effective in letting you identify unclear **transitions** from one idea to another and **vague wording.**

Of course, if you can set aside a draft for several days before rereading, all the better. Most writing situations, especially in the workplace, don't allow much luxury of time; but it's the rare document that must be delivered the same day it's assigned. Whenever a writer knows of a deadline in advance, even a few days, that writer would be well advised to draft sufficiently before the deadline to make use of wait time.

Looking through the Reader's Eyes

Using wait time to gain perspective on a draft is necessary for strong revision, but it won't help much if you aren't able to see the draft from something close to the perspective that a primary reader of the text would have. The next technique we will describe is how to get good, direct feedback from readers themselves. Since all writers have to be critics of their own work, it's vital that writers be able to "be"—at least imagine themselves to be—those readers.

Some ways to increase your empathy with readers include:

1. *Studying documents of the same kind you are composing:* Good writers in any genre are almost always avid, studious readers of the same type of work, whether novels or letters to the editor or crime reports or play reviews. As described under Formatting, finding and studying files of similar documents definitely helps in the writing process. If finding such files is difficult, ask the person who assigned you the writing task if samples are available.

2. *Doing the audience analysis exercise* (under Drafting for the Audience): In the log or elsewhere, do one or more writings to help put you in the reader's frame of mind. Consider such questions as "What does my reader wish to get out of this reading?" "What will my reader expect to see first?" "What would be likely to grab my reader's interest?" "What should I avoid in order to keep my reader from getting upset or bored?"

3. *Keeping handy the checklists of format, audience, and purpose criteria:* The more you work with lists of criteria, such as those given in these categories in the Drafting section, the more you will instinctively apply these criteria. While you are still relatively new at working with a particular kind of assignment, it's important to keep at hand your carefully annotated assignment, log writings about audience expectations, and other notes.

Getting Good Feedback from Readers

Especially in facing assignments in new genres or in writing for new audiences, experienced writers have learned how indispensable feedback from knowledgeable sources is to good rewriting. Carefully using wait time and keeping handy any written criteria always help produce better prose, but there is no substitute for specific advice from:

1. Readers for whom the document is intended
2. Other writers experienced in that genre or with that type of reader
3. Another writer whose opinions you trust to be careful and honest

Reader 1, also known as the **primary audience,** should never be presumed to be inaccessible or unwilling to comment on a draft. For example, although college faculty in most courses do not mandate nor even formally invite students to request feedback (though such invitations have become more common), almost all faculty are open to such requests from students and appreciate their initiative and seriousness in making the request. Conversely, while magazine editors may not offer to comment on drafts per se, the process by which articles are considered for publication usually means feedback and revision by the writer. Most material submitted to academic journals, for example, is neither accepted nor rejected outright; editors routinely send writers fairly substantial commentary written by themselves and by members of the editorial board, and these responses enable revision by the writer.

Another kind of primary reader is a **member of a larger public** who will be receiving a document and who will be expected to act in some way on its message. Everything from course syllabi to news releases to advertising is meant for such readers. You should avoid characterizing such audiences in the mass as "general readers" or the like; instead, think of each hypothetical reader as an individual, with identifiable needs and characteristics. If at all possible, get feedback on a draft from one or more members of that readership. As with the first type of primary reader, give such readers specific questions that will focus commentary and show them that you want concrete suggestions—not vague praise.

Reader 2, the **writer with experience in that genre or with that audience,** can be invaluable in pointing out handy tricks and hidden pitfalls. When asking for feedback from such a source, be sure to specify exactly why you are seeking this person's advice (e.g., "I read your review and I know you've had a lot of experience writing these. Will you read my draft and point out some things I should be sure to do and some things I should be sure to avoid?"). Because of this writer's experience, you can rely on his or her awareness of most of the concerns you may have about format, audience, and purpose; moreover, this writer will be aware of other concerns that may not have crossed your mind. Be ready to listen, to answer questions this writer will pose to *you* about format and other issues, and take careful notes.

Reader 3, the **trusted adviser,** will be valuable to you mainly for his/ her candor, the ability to write well him- or herself, and knowledge of how to communicate clearly with you. It usually takes much practice in asking for feedback, perhaps years, for a writer to identify a person with these qualities.

Don't confuse a trusted writing adviser with a close relative or good friend. A relative or friend *might* turn out to be a good writing adviser, but it will take time for you to find that out. Never turn to anyone for advice just because that person is convenient to you or might feel obligated to give you some kind of response.

Some All-Purpose Rules for Getting Feedback

Regardless of the reader or the situation, a few good practices in getting good feedback pertain:

1. *Always ask specific questions.* Before showing your work to someone, spend a few minutes writing several questions that will help your respondent focus commentary. Suggestions: Mark passages that you found especially difficult to write and write out why you are concerned about the wording; ask the all-purpose questions "Where do I need to explain in more detail?" "Where should I cut?"

2. *Make it clear to your informant that you want constructive suggestions, not a pat on the back.* The least useful question to ask a respondent is "What do you think?" Unless the informant knows you well and knows that you really want honest, critical feedback, the respondent's tendency will be to make a generalized "feel good" comment that won't help you revise at all.

If you really do need some encouragement—and all writers do—ask the informant what, if anything, is strong in the draft and why. Then move on and ask your specific questions to spark definite suggestions for change.

3. *Listen carefully, take notes, and exercise judgment.* Your attitude to criticism should always be open, but it's also important to maintain integrity, respect for your own judgment. Listen respectfully to every reader's commentary, take notes on and beside your draft, but don't rush to change the draft until you have carefully weighed each comment. Even readers with similar backgrounds will rarely concur on all, even most, suggestions, so you should rely on wait time and on your heightened awareness of format, audience, and purpose in order to decide how much critical commentary to follow.

4. *Get more than one opinion.* If you read the Preface to this book, you will notice that reviews of drafts of this guide have been sought from several people, all of them highly regarded in composition studies or in theatre. While it isn't usually practical for writers in most school or workplace situations to ask a wide range of opinions, strive to avoid giving too much weight to one person's response—especially if that person is other than the professor who will be grading the school assignment or the supervisor who will be judging the proposal. Getting more than one opinion will let you see if a person's judgment is merely idiosyncratic. Reinforcing comments from several readers will give you confidence in the changes you plan to make.

Caution: While getting more than one opinion on your draft is usually advisable, you may not need to if the first person you consult is either your primary reader or the most knowledgeable person on that type of document. Especially in workplace settings, you should avoid the risk of insulting a senior colleague by "shopping around" for writing advice after you've received feedback from that person.

Some All-Purpose Questions to Ask Readers

Remember that the questions you spend time writing about your draft, format, audiences, and purposes will be the best questions. Nevertheless, here are a few that work in most writing situations:

1. *What is my main point here? What do you feel I'm mainly trying to accomplish?*
2. *What do you think I should write more about? What needs further explanation?*
3. *What could be cut? Why?*
4. *How would you characterize the person I seem to be writing for? Could you suggest any shift in my sense of the reader?*

5. *What words or phrases seem to you unclear or misleading? Where are you confused?*
6. *What questions do you have for me about the draft?*

Note that all of these questions must be answered with information, not a simple judgment of "yes"/"no," "okay"/"could be better." Your questions should show the reader that you expect to revise and need substantive help in identifying where and how to change.

EDITING THE REVISED DRAFT

Writers differ in their ways of attending to matters of formatting, grammar (syntax), punctuation, and spelling in the drafting and revision stages. Some writers need to keep everything neat and correct as they compose; misspellings, typos, and other minor mistakes distract their thinking. Others write first, then tidy up the details just before they submit the document to the primary reader. Some writers do some of both.

Whatever the variations, most experienced writers give their revised drafts an **editing review** before submitting them to the reader. This pattern is exemplified in book publishing, wherein the revised typescript is carefully **copyedited** only after all changes have been made in the ideas (content) and organization of the work. Then, once the copyedited text is set into page proofs (the actual typeset sheets in the type font and size in which they will appear to the public), it is **proofread** at least once more to ensure that all errors have been caught (some are never caught, of course).

The final section of this chapter will deal with a few common errors in **grammar, punctuation,** and **spelling** within what linguists call **Standard Edited American English.** SEAE is the specialized dialect of written English used in American schools, government, and business. As with all dialects, this one is continually changing, so don't be surprised to see occasional exceptions to these "rules" in some documents.

This chapter in no way substitutes for a comprehensive **handbook of English grammar and usage,** such as *The Allyn and Bacon Handbook.* This chapter will only alert you to a few of the *most* common errors that irk teachers, clients, supervisors, and other readers.

Three Common Errors in Grammar and Usage

Subject/Verb Disagreement

Rule: If the subject of a sentence is singular, the verb must be singular; if the subject is plural, the verb must be plural.

Wrong   The *Redwings is* the team that represents our town in the tournament.

Right   The *Redwings are* the team that represents our town in the tournament.

Wrong   The full *collection* of books, monographs, and letters *reside* in the university library.

Right   The full *collection* of books, articles, and letters *resides* in the university library.

Vague Pronoun Reference

Rule: In order to avoid confusing the reader, writers should avoid using a pronoun to substitute for a group of nouns not in a simple series. Readers will tend not to know to which noun(s) the pronoun is referring.

Wrong   The Edict of 1245 superseded the Decree of 1218, *which* meant that residents of the kingdom had to register for taxation according to the value of land and livestock.

Right   The Edict of 1245 superseded the Decree of 1218; the Edict requiring that residents of the kingdom register for taxation according to the value of land and livestock.

Sentence Fragments

Rule: The subject of a sentence may not be a demonstrative pronoun (*which, that, who*), unless the sentence is phrased as a question.

Wrong   Directing is a collaborative process. *Which* sometimes makes the director's work difficult to evaluate.

Right   Directing is a collaborative process, which sometimes makes the director's work difficult to evaluate.

Two Common Errors in Punctuation

Comma Splice or Fault

Rule: A comma should not be used as connecting punctuation between two complete sentences.

Wrong   The company tried TQM during the early 1980s, it downsized drastically in the early 1990s and began outsourcing its training and accounting.

Right   The company tried TQM during the early 1980s; it downsized drastically in the early 1990s and began outsourcing its training and accounting.

Right   The company tried TQM during the early 1980s, *then* it down-sized drastically in the early 1990s and began outsourcing its training and accounting.

Lack of the Second Comma in a Nonrestrictive Noun Phrase or Clause

Rule: When a comma is used at the beginning of a noun phrase or clause, a second comma must be used to close the phrase or clause (except when the phrase or clause ends the sentence).

Wrong   *Their Eyes Were Watching God,* a book by Zora Neale Hurston was widely criticized and ignored when first published but has become popular in recent years.

Right   *Their Eyes Were Watching God,* a book by Zora Neale Hurston, was widely criticized and ignored when first published but has become popular in recent years.

Two Common Spelling Errors

Misuse of the Spell-Checker (e.g., with homophones)

While the spell-check function of most word processing programs will catch many spelling errors during the composition process, many writers either forget to use the spell-checker or rely on it to do things it cannot. For example, a spell-checker will not be able to pick up **wrong usage** of a **homophone** (a word that sounds like another but means something different). The most common so-called "spelling" errors are actually uses of the wrong homophone (*it's* instead of *its*, *their* instead of *they're* or *there*). So you will need to proofread your documents carefully for uses of these words, even if you use a spell-checker for other purposes.

Hint: If you know that homophones give you problems and if your word processing program allows you to do this, try **removing from your spell-checker's dictionary** the homophones that plague your writing. In this way, every use of the problematic words will be marked by your program so that you may review the spellings. Some commonly misused homophones:

it's/its	their/they're/there	flier/flyer
affect/effect	discrete/discreet	site/cite/sight
here/hear		

and a near-homophone: lose/loose

The Problem with Spelling by Sound: The Schwa

The most common *kind* of English sound that is misspelled is the **vowel in an unaccented syllable.** Try saying the following three words: *tendon, independent, pennant.*

Notice that the final syllable of each word has the *same* vowel sound, but that a different vowel is used in each case; *tendon, independent, pennant.* This vowel sound is called by linguists the **schwa,** represented in the phonetic alphabet by the symbol ə, a character not present in English spelling. Chances are that if you consider yourself a poor speller, a significant proportion of your spelling errors occur with schwas, because the correct vowel is not determined by sound.

Fortunately, spell-checkers are great at picking up most schwa errors (except in a homophone such as *effect/affect*), so use the spell-checker. However, if you are not word-processing a document and if you don't trust your spelling, pay particular attention to those unaccented vowels and consult the dictionary.

A Final Note on Proofreading

Proofreading is no fun for most writers. To do it well, you must disregard *what* you have written about and pay *precise* attention to the tiniest details of appearance. Many readers place extremely high importance on correct syntax, punctuation, and spelling; even one error is sometimes enough to ruin the strong impression created by your careful predraft efforts, drafting, and revision. Consequently, careful proofreading is an absolute must for any document with which you want to win a reader's interest and good will, so time in the writing process must be reserved for this final, equally important stage.

Proofreading for Spelling Errors

If you are not writing on a word processor with a spell-check program, the best way to check for spelling errors is the tedious but effective technique of **reading your text backward one word at a time.** In this way, you can concentrate on each word because you will not get caught up in the flow of ideas. But remember to stay alert for misused **homophones** (see under Misuse of the Spell-Checker); remember, too, that this technique only works for spelling—it can't help you catch any other kind of error. (See the Editing section for other tips on checking for spelling errors.)

Proofreading for Errors in Punctuation and Syntax

See the Editing section and keep it handy when proofing your documents. The common errors noted there are often missed by even the most sophisticated grammar-checking programs on computer word processors. Nevertheless, we strongly recommend the most recent versions of such grammar-checking programs because they are adept at catching such common errors as repetition of the same word (*in in*), too much spacing between words, wrong punctuation, and the frequent failure of writers to remember that a change in one part of a sentence means that they must change other parts of the sentence in order for syntax to be consistent. For example, it's common for a writer to change a plural noun to a singular noun and forget to change the corresponding verb.

But **use grammar-checkers cautiously.** Not only do they miss much more than they pick up, but they also alert the writer to many possible errors that are in fact correct constructions. So tend to trust your own judgment more than the computer's. The best editors are human; in any workplace where correct writing is important, good editors are worth their weight in gold.

4

THE THEATRE REVIEW AND DRAMATIC CRITICISM

There you are, in the dark, in a crowded theatre, as an unfamiliar play hurtles past you. Your attention is riveted as an actor makes a startling, effective gesture: Who is he and what character is he playing? The stage image coalesces around a pair of silent lovers, telling their inner story in the vocabulary of light, shadow, and color: Who did that? What are their names? The plot takes an unexpected turn, hinging on a key revelation: What was the information, who brought it, and why is it important? You look around at your fellow theatregoers, who sit engrossed in the performance blissfully unconcerned about these details, while you are hard at work attempting to fix each one in your mind for later recall and use.

Why can't you simply sit back and enjoy the show? Because you are a **theatre reviewer,** responsible to your readers and to the creators of the performance for an accurate, insightful, and compelling account of the evening's events. You're watching everything through eyes that are partly a journalist's and partly a scholar's. You'll make a report of the play and production, but you'll also analyze it, interpret it, serve as a medium between the artwork and its potential audience.

Or you may be a **scholar of dramatic literature,** attempting to enhance your experience of the literary text through witness and analysis of the text as it comes alive on the stage. You realize that drama is essentially a performance medium; you cannot obtain a rich sense of the nuances of the text without thinking intently about how the text relates to the many facets of live theatre.

This chapter describes the process of **active listening and viewing** of theatre performance; it goes on to show how to write effectively about that experience for diverse readers. The skills of close observation of theatre needed by reviewer and scholar are very similar; the student of dramatic literature should be able easily to adapt to his or her writing about plays the techniques we offer here for those writing theatre reviews.

Observing and analyzing live performance is hard but important work—for the reasons we suggested in Chapter 1, the capturing of moments in the life of an art form that would otherwise be fleeting—and in this chapter you will discover some techniques that make the job both possible and pleasurable.

REVIEWERS AND CRITICS

First, a word about terms. Theatre reviews are often written by people called **drama critics,** but to preserve the clarity of the distinction between text and performance, we will mostly use the term *theatre* to refer to the performed play and *drama* to refer to the text. The difference between a review and a piece of criticism is more subtle; a review tends to be shorter, less analytical, and more immediate to the event it is describing, whereas the term *criticism* implies a longer, more thoughtful, and less time-sensitive response to the work. The same imprecise distinction can be made between the writers themselves, the *reviewer* and the *critic.* In practice, however, the two terms overlap so fluidly that they tend to be interchangeable, and we will mostly use them that way.

THE SHAPE OF A REVIEW

Theatre reviews change shape and purpose depending on their audience. For this discussion, let's consider three basic venues: the **newspaper,** the **magazine,** and the **journal.**

Writing for Newspapers

The reader of a daily newspaper wants a review to appear as promptly after opening night as possible. The opening of a new production is, after all, a newsworthy event in a community, just like the premiere of a film or the results of a ball game.

The reader wants to know the particulars of the event and also hungers for some insight that goes deeper than the mere facts. This combination of information and analysis is expressed by journalists in the formula **5 w's and an h:** *who, what, when, where, why,* and *how.* A good news story answers those questions, and a good play review might do well to use the scheme as a point of departure.

Who produced the play? What was it about? When does it perform? These questions cover the basic facts of the case. Why did the company choose the play, and why did they interpret it as they did? How effective was the interpretation? These latter questions speak to the critic's judgment of the success or failure of the production, and may serve to help the reader make an informed decision about whether or not to attend the show.

Writing for Magazines

Magazine readers, receiving their weekly issue of, for example, *Time, The Nation, The New Yorker,* or *The New Republic,* are more interested in implications of the event that go beyond the reach of a local theatre. Is this production a significant new interpretation of a classic text? Is it the premiere of an interesting new play? Does the play or the production address some important theme in contemporary society? Is there a production element—the direction, the acting, the design—that makes an interesting advancement in the art form? The majority of magazine readers are unlikely ever to see the production they are reading about, and so the review has to make a claim for their attention based on more than local interest or a ticket-buyer's decision.

Writing for Scholarly Journals

Journals (such as *The Hudson Review, The American Scholar,* or *New Theatre Quarterly*) that focus on scholarship, culture, politics, or some other general area of interest, tend to appear quarterly, semiannually, or annually. A play review for a journal should take the long view, placing the play or production in a larger context of similar events, commenting on its contribution to the life of its times, assessing its potential impact on the drama (or, in exceptional cases, on society itself). Here the occasion of the production is a springboard for the critic's commentary rather than the primary focus; the *why* and *how* come to the foreground, supported by the minimum necessary armature of other details.

SUITING THE REVIEW TO THE AUDIENCE: THE THREE ELEMENTS

Almost all dramatic criticism is organized around a blend of **reportage, analysis,** and **judgment.** The relative balance of each element changes with the intended audience: a newspaper review may favor reportage and judgment ("This is what it is; this is what I think about it"), while a magazine or journal article may downplay some of the local particulars in order to emphasize analysis and judgment of a more complex nature ("These are the implications of the work as I see them; this is why I think it is an important work").

There is no hard-and-fast rule about the balance of the three elements to use when crafting a review for a given audience. Some newspaper critics weave insightful analysis throughout their reportage, while some journals favor a heavy dose of factual reporting at the expense of critical judgment. The individual critic must determine the proper weight for each element in a review.

Some of that determination will be dictated by the nature of the event itself. A new play may require more reportage simply to capture the unfamiliar subject matter; a classic may invite more analysis of its treatment of familiar themes; a production with unusual sets or costumes will compel the critic to spend more time considering those features.

The First Element: Reportage

Reportage provides the basic data of the event: "Shakespeare's *Twelfth Night* opened last night at the Superior Repertory Theater, directed by Olivia Orsino. The production, with sets and costumes by Andrew Tobias and lighting by Maria Viola, is scheduled to play nightly except Mondays through April 23. The cast includes. . . . "

Such a paragraph deals efficiently with the journalist's *who/what/where/ when* questions, postponing the all-important *why* and *how,* which belong more to the element of **analysis.** It has a deliberately journalistic flavor and as such might be used unchanged in the beginning of a newspaper review. The information it contains would also appear in a magazine or journal, but dispersed throughout the article as the critic pauses to analyze the various elements of production.

You'll note a careful avoidance of adjectives—how easily one could slip "stunning" or "tedious" in front of almost any element of the paragraph— because the informative purpose of these sentences is not helped by unsupported assertions about quality. In crafting reportage, the critic wants to lay out the facts for the reader in as objective a manner as possible, saving analysis for a later portion of the review.

Naming Names

One stylistic dilemma faced by every critic is how to credit all the artists involved in the production in a graceful manner. A common practice is to cite the name of the artist in connection with the first mention of his or her role, perhaps in a summary of the plot: "Sebastian (Allen Burbage) comes

ashore accompanied by his faithful companion, Antonio (John Benson) . . ."
Some reviewers add an evaluative phrase: "Sebastian (sensitively played
by Allen Burbage). . . ." This technique is common in journalistic reviewing
because it saves space and time, but it often creates more questions than it
answers unless some detail in support of the "sensitivity" of the performance is offered later in the review. Use these judgments sparingly!

Directors and designers can be credited in the body of the review in the
same way: "The lighting, by Craig Gordon, relies on pale tints and shim-
mering effects to create a sense of fragility. . . ." Note the avoidance of an
adjective ("The *magnificent* lighting, by Craig Gordon . . .") in favor of a
phrase that describes the effect of the artist's work.

Cast and Staff Lists.   It is often impossible to mention every artist in the
body copy of the review; to do so for a large-cast play would create an un-
manageable burden both in length and style. Many newspapers solve this
problem by including a complete cast and staff list either at the beginning
of the review (cf. the *New York Times*) or by running a list at the end of all
those who were not mentioned in the body of the piece (cf. the *Washington
Post*). Either method serves to guarantee that the journalistic mandate of the
first *w*—the all-important *who*—is fulfilled.

A Reportage Checklist
Beyond the journalist's four w's, the critic should also endeavor to describe
the **particulars of the production,** paying attention to at least *some* of the
following elements in a nonjudgmental, reportorial style:

- *Text:* plot, major characters, main idea, effectiveness of language, other
  elements (such as music)
- *Setting:* physical appearance, materials, style, color, relationship to the
  theatre's architecture, relationship to the play
- *Costumes:* choice of period, color, materials, style, relationship to the
  characters and the play
- *Lighting:* atmosphere created, color choices, style, enhancement of (or
  detraction from) the mood of the piece
- *Sound:* function of sound effects or musical score; specific examples of
  sound that support or compete with action
- *Acting:* clarity of characterizations, vocal and physical work, notable
  moments in performance, sense of ensemble playing
- *Directing:* clarity of story, casting choices, tempo and rhythm of performance, composition of stage images

It should be apparent that answering every item on the checklist would
create a very long and extraordinarily dull review. The best use for the list

is as a memory aid for the dummy draft stage of writing (see Chapter 3 for an explanation of this term) to make sure that your reportage covers the **key elements appropriate for this production and your review of it.** Consult your list before and after viewing the production.

Reportage in Action

A draft description of the visual elements of a particular moment might go into great detail:

> The coastline where Sebastian and the Sailor come ashore is represented by a silver strand of fabric, suspended at waist level by two costumed stagehands who gently undulate the fabric, seemingly to create an effect of gentle surf and sea breezes. The lighting supports this image through a wash of cool light from a low side angle, as if moonlight were being reflected off the waves and sand. A light wisp of fog occasionally moves across the stage, eddying and swirling around the actors' feet and over the buff-colored, dappled floor cloth. Sebastian wears a faded grey overcoat that places him in color harmony with the entire seacoast image, and in fact renders him nearly indistinguishable from his surroundings at times.

Some or all of this material might find its way into the review, but writing it out helps the critic discover what will become important, and creates a reservoir of description from which to draw as the review takes final form.

There are elements of reportage that blur the line between description and analysis. Recognizing that, make an effort to stick to *observable phenomena* at this point in your writing. An actor or a director may make a strong statement with a gesture, a vocal inflection, or a choice of stage composition. In the sample paragraph, the temptation to include words and phrases like "eerily compelling," "subtle," "mesmerizing," and so forth, was very strong. For reportage, again, it is best to try to record the choices as they are, saving your analysis of their effectiveness (and your qualitative adjectives) for later.

The Second Element: Analysis

If you've done the hard work of reportage, analysis comes more easily, since you'll be dealing with specific **images, moments,** and **ideas.** The purpose of your analytical work is to assess the intentions and effectiveness of the production in such a way that the reader is brought to a clearer understanding of the artistic ambitions of the play and production. Put another way, the critic's next step is to ask: "What is the production's *attempt?* What are the writer, director, actors, and designers trying to create and to what end?"

To Interview or Not to Interview?

In some cases, the reviewer is in a position simply to *ask* the artists these questions directly, but a blurring of the lines between feature reporting and true criticism can occur when the critic interviews the creators of the work under discussion. Critics traditionally place themselves in the position of an idealized, well-informed audience member, one without special access to the inner workings of the artists' minds **except as those workings are revealed in the art itself.**

Here the critic's imagination must enter the field. In the sample description the set, lights, and costumes were described in some detail, and a certain effect was hinted at. Now the critic can move into the more subjective realm of analysis by suggesting a reason, a thought, an **intention** for the imagery, selecting only those details that signify this intention, and recasting the idea as follows:

> Sebastian wears a faded grey overcoat that so completely harmonizes with the moonlit surroundings that he seems, ghost-like, to slip from visibility from time to time, fading almost completely into the night mists. It is as if he were present and absent simultaneously, always there and just arrived, a dream-vision and a material reality in alternate moments. The staging creates a metaphor for the crisis of Sebastian's separation from his twin sister, Viola, and foreshadows their impending reunion.

In this example the critic uses the materials of reportage but adds an interpretive guess about the **reason** for or the **intention** of the director and designers' choices—namely, the creation of a metaphor and an image rooted in the plot of the play. There is still no hint of a final evaluative opinion on these choices.

It would be easy, however, to include qualitative adjectives in this analysis. For example, the metaphor might be "insightful" or "heavy handed," depending on the critic's personal evaluation of the moment; in the same vein, "hauntingly" or "clumsily" might be inserted before "foreshadows their impending reunion." Weaving qualitative adjectives in and around substantive analysis is one way of saving time and space in a review and, if done carefully, can be a graceful way to lead the reader toward the critic's ultimate judgment. The important thing is to provide the reader with enough specific description and analysis that whatever adjectives are chosen serve to illuminate the critic's point of view without obscuring the artist's.

The Third Element: Judgment

Any discussion of intention in a work of art invites two follow-up questions: Was the intention realized, and was it a worthwhile intention in the first place? In the answer to that second question we come to the third leg of our critical tripod, the **judgments** a critic makes on the ultimate effectiveness and worth of a play or production.

A critic might look at the moment described in the following schematic way:

1. The director intended to create a metaphor for Sebastian and Viola's separation anxiety through blending Sebastian into his environment, so that his presence took on a ghostly quality.
2. This intention was realized, in that Sebastian seemed to disappear or dissolve at certain moments through the use of coordinated design elements, effectively creating a ghostly image and foreshadowing the twins' reunion.
3. This intention was worthwhile, in that it created an emotional context of incompleteness and immateriality that was only removed when the twins are reunited, thus intensifying our feelings for both Sebastian and Viola.

This mental schematic could then be rendered into readable prose as a continuation of the review paragraph:

> . . . Sebastian's ghostly, never-quite-all-there appearance clings to him until the moment of reunion with his twin sister, which makes the audience feel something of the sense of incompleteness, hunger, and loss that the twins themselves must have felt—and the corresponding satisfaction and relief when the bond is reestablished. Through visual insights such as this, Superior Repertory's production of *Twelfth Night* finds a deeper emotional core beneath the obvious comedy than is usually the case.

Conversely, a critic seeing the same production but finding the moment as described in disharmony with the tonality of the text as a whole might agree with steps 1 and 2 of the schematic but might revise step 3 as follows:

3. The intention was not worthwhile, in that it created a too-serious, even solemn undertone to the twins' relationship; this exaggerated solemnity made the subsequent comedy of their relationships with others seem like an intrusion.

This critic might extend the paragraph as follows:

These aesthetically pleasing and carefully wrought design values, unfortunately, are placed in service of what seems a misguided vision of the play: that the dark undercurrents of separation and loss are more important to Shakespeare than the insistent themes of reconciliation and harmony that resound throughout the language of the piece, creating a production that is, in effect, at war with its own better self.

The Critic's Individual Vision

Both of our imaginary critics have essentially agreed on the reportage and analysis of the moment; they diverge in their judgment of it. Here is where the individuality and the art of criticism make themselves felt. Critics bring different tastes, experiences, and prejudices to the theatre; it may not be an exaggeration to say that even from night to night a single critic's response to a given production might vary.

The essential point is that **reportage** and **analysis** must precede **judgment** in the thought process of a responsible critic. The goal must be to **see** accurately, **describe** fully, **think** clearly, and then (and only then) to **judge** fairly the merits of the work.

"CRITICAL MASS": ACHIEVING EFFECTIVE ARGUMENT IN THE REVIEW

In the dummy draft stage of your writing (see Chapter 3), it is helpful to follow the order of events outlined here. In the subsequent rough draft and later revisions, you can begin to integrate analysis with reportage more seamlessly and to incorporate your critical judgments throughout the piece.

A reader will easily accept evaluative adjectives and expressions of critical opinion anywhere in a review as long as a state of affairs that we might call **critical mass** has been reached: *that moment when the reader feels that judgment is adequately supported by evidence.*

Some professional critics make a practice of leading with a statement of opinion in the first paragraph, and then proceeding to demonstrate why it is valid; others withhold their judgment until they've established a groundwork of evidence. Both approaches can yield satisfying reviews. Behind both is the reportage–analysis–judgment process, closer to the surface in the latter approach, further in the background in the former.

Yes/No/Maybe

Judgments in reviews need not be total, irrevocable, and absolute. Often a production creates mixed meanings (and mixed feelings), or is successful in realizing certain intentions while missing others. A good critic will respond to this unsettled state of affairs with a review that credits the successes while not ignoring the failures. Then, too, the critic may feel uncertain about some of the points the production is attempting to make; that uncertainty, freely and intelligently discussed, can become a useful framework for a review, as long as the critic does the necessary work of reportage and analysis before confessing an inability to make a final judgment.

Durability

A great drama review remains interesting to read long after the production has faded from memory. We cherish good critics because they accomplish three things: they report the event evocatively, analyze its essence and its execution, and make judgments about its ultimate quality and endurance. In so doing, they contribute a valuable record to the ongoing dialogue of culture: the encounter of bright minds with powerful moments, the capture of a fleeting insight that would otherwise be, in Robert Brustein's evocative phrase, "written on the wind."

THE PRACTICAL CRITIC: A FEW HINTS

Theatre reviewing and dramatic criticism are a blend of art and craft. The process of perception and analysis suggested in the preceding pages will help develop the critic's art; the following checklist is offered as a guide to some of the issues of craft that the field invites.

- **Reading the play:** Most critics prefer to read the play before reviewing a production; this allows for comparisons between the critic's and director's perspectives on the text. In the case of a new or unpublished text, it is sometimes possible to secure a reading copy from the theatre. If not, the best advice is: listen hard.
- **Taking notes (1):** For some thoughts about the role of note taking in writing, refer back to Chapter 2. The following are some hints for the special challenges of the drama critic. You will have to take some notes in the dark while you watch the play, so get a small or medium-sized notebook with a spiral binding across the top—a steno pad works well. Use a roller-ball or other quiet pen with an easy flow of ink; pencils are too noisy and break too often, and felt-tip pens can also be noisy and too smudgy. Write larger than normal, since you won't be looking at what you write while you're writing. Move down the page consciously and freely; more than one critic has written six or seven lines over each other, only to find one big horizontal smudge when the show's over.

- **Taking notes (2):** If it's a new and unpublished play, you might need to transcribe some key dialogue word for word; otherwise, get a copy of the script and use that for quotations after the fact.
- **Taking notes (3):** Your notes should highlight moments you need to remember in detail. Our mythical *Twelfth Night* critic might have scribbled "seacoast—fabric strip/waves—low sidelight—Sebastian as grey ghost" during the performance, then fleshed out the idea immediately following the show, or the next day. Trust yourself to watch the play and understand the story; don't take notes on every plot point. If an actor does something unusual or extraordinary, note the character and the moment, but don't take time during the performance to write a detailed description. Your notes will jog your memory later, when you can take the time to recollect in detail.
- **Keeping the program or playbill:** Every theatre publishes at least a simple cast and staff list; make sure you get one, and use it for accurate spellings and as a checklist to make sure you've thought about all the component parts of the production. You may see a listing for a particular artist that reminds you of an important moment in the play. If your review format requires a complete listing of the artists, either as a headnote, endnote, or distributed through your piece, here is your definitive source.
- **Letting a little time pass—but not too much:** The professional newspaper critic is the first one up the aisle at the end of a performance and often is writing on a deadline a few hours away. Unless that pressure is forced upon you, wait about a day before sitting down at the keyboard to begin your dummy draft. If you've taken good notes, you'll find that your impressions of the production will be easy to recall, and the passage of a little time will help you focus on the elements that really matter. If too much time elapses, however, you will find yourself too dependent on your notes, and the review may lack the richness of detail that it needs.
- **Considering the audience before beginning your draft:** Chapter 3 of this book discusses the role of the reader (under Drafting for Your Audience) in some detail; think about your reader as you work out the proper balance of reportage, analysis, and judgment for your review.
- And finally, because it bears repeating, **following the effective progression: Report** before you analyze; **analyze** before you judge; and **judge** based on your reportage and analysis.

5

TEXT ANALYSIS

CONNECTING THE STAGE AND THE STUDY

There are many reasons to sit down with a play in one hand, figuratively speaking, and a blank sheet of paper in the other, with the goal in mind of writing a textual analysis. In the academic world, drama is subject to the same kinds of literary criticism as poems, novels, and short stories, and plays are often included in literature survey courses. In the world of practical theatre, artists develop production ideas based on their analyses of the dramatic text.

As we indicated in Chapter 1, however, play analysis for the study and the stage have too often been seen as separate, one belonging to the play as literature and one to the performed work of theatre. In fact, the two are inseparable, and though the results may differ in the form they ultimately take, the intellectual effort required is much the same. If a distinction needs to be made, it is between the techniques used for looking at the play in either of its modes and those applied to the analysis of nonperforming types of literature.

THE TEXT AS BLUEPRINT FOR PRODUCTION

Our basic premise is that the dramatic text—the script—should be seen as a **blueprint for production** rather than as a finished piece of art in its own right. A play is closer in essence to a musical score than to a novel; all three documents are subject to analysis on the page, but the play and the score remain incomplete without the interpretive art of the performer, while the novel requires only the "private performance" of the individual reader.

LITERARY ANALYSIS AND FUNCTIONAL ANALYSIS

Speaking broadly, a play analysis project may take two major forms as a final outcome, and the choice will depend, like so many decisions in writing, on the audience for the work. One form calls for *an examination of a play's themes, images, language, context,* or some other defining characteristic of the work. We'll call this kind of paper a **literary analysis,** since it will most often be required in a dramatic literature course or a survey course that includes drama as one of its components.

Production-oriented courses such as those in directing, acting, or design may be less concerned with a formal exposition of the play's literary values and more interested in mining the text for the *information and inspiration required to develop a production plan.* This kind of writing can be called **functional analysis,** since it results in a set of notes or a paper that describes how some aspects of a play work.

As you will see later in the chapter, the thought required for both kinds of analysis remains the same until a fairly late point in the process. The paths diverge at (or just after) the creation of the dummy draft. (See Chapter 3 for an explanation of this term.)

THE AUDIENCE, REAL AND IMAGINARY

Although the real audience for a play analysis of either kind is likely to be the professor who makes the assignment, it is sometimes helpful to imagine a broader audience for the work. One imaginary audience for a **literary analysis** of drama might be the readers of an anthology of drama; the paper might serve as an introduction to the chosen play or group of plays for the general reader in an academic setting.

The audience for a **functional analysis** might be imagined as the collaborative team of artists engaged in an actual production. Indeed, in this day of far-flung collaborators in the professional theatre, a functional analysis might have quite a practical impact when transmitted by e-mail from a director in Chicago to a set designer in New York, a lighting designer in San Diego, a costume designer in Seattle, and a dramaturg in Tallahassee!

THE SPECIAL CHARACTERISTICS OF PLAYS

Quite obviously, the format and style of the two kinds of analysis will differ significantly. The literary analysis will be formally constructed, along the lines of a term paper, while the functional analysis might take the form of a series of extended, detailed notes.

Both kinds of writing, however, proceed from the fundamental assumption that a dramatic text is best understood in its own terms rather than those of prose fiction or poetry. Therefore, the special characteristics that make a play a springboard or blueprint for performance will be a primary concern in what follows. We make no claim to offer a comprehensive theory of drama in this chapter, but rather we suggest a method for working with the preponderance of plays that students are likely to encounter either in the study or on the stage.

What Makes a Play?

It's an age-old question, of course, grappled with at least as far back as Aristotle's *Poetics* (4th cen. B.C.E). Philosophers at that time were concerned with differentiating drama from other current forms, such as the epic poem typified by Homer's *Iliad* and *Odyssey*. Aristotle, whose philosophical method was grounded in the natural sciences, was a skilled taxonomist, adept at arranging things by categories and classes. Naturally, he wished to separate literary works for closer analysis much as he might classify plant species or the various kinds of argumentation. Aristotle's famous definition of tragedy is worth excerpting here because it contains several terms which still help distinguish a play from any other kind of artistic creation:

> Tragedy, then, is an imitation of an action that is serious, complete, and of a certain magnitude; in language pleasurably embellished with each kind of artistic ornament . . . in the form of action, not of narrative . . . Every tragedy must have six parts, which parts determine its quality — namely, Plot, Characters, Diction, Intellect, Song, and Spectacle.[*]

Students of Aristotle will notice immediately that we have omitted the famous reference to the purgation of pity and terror, or *catharsis*, since its meaning is a subject of lively and ongoing scholarly debate, and its application to the present discussion is tangential. The key word here is **action.** Aristotle insists on the distinction between action and narrative, and he rates **plot** as the most important of the six elements of tragedy (as he does for comedy as well, elsewhere in his writings).

Though a number of alternative organizing principles for drama and theatre have emerged in the centuries since Aristotle wrote—including the principle of no organizing principle—the vast majority of plays continue to be based on the idea of **action.** When a character in Samuel Beckett's *Endgame* says, "Something is taking its course," he is describing, in terms both definitively modern and distinctly Aristotelian, the essential role of action in drama.

---

[*]*Poetics*, trans. S. H. Butcher (London: MacMillan, 1895).

The Life of an Action

In most plays, the story unfolds through a series of interlocking actions. We come to know the plot and the characters (Aristotle's top two elements) through the pattern of what they *do* as much as by what they *say*. Actions form the heartbeat of a play. When they come into conflict with each other, the dramatic pulse quickens. When they're all resolved, or declared impossible to resolve, the play is over (or ought to be).

What makes an action dramatic? In many of the most popular motion pictures of our time, "action" is one of the primary attractions—as buildings, airplanes, railroad trains, people, cities, and alien spacecraft blow up in ever-more-colorful fireballs. We might hear a gasped "Wow! That was dramatic!" from the row behind us, followed by the soft pitter-patter of spilled popcorn hitting the theatre floor.

Spectacular effects alone, however, do not make an action dramatic (notice the last-place finish of **spectacle** on Aristotle's list). To create a dramatic action, the artist sets in motion the following chain reaction:

Motive + obstacle + consequence = drama

A **motive** exists when an action is undertaken for a reason; a character wants something (which is sometimes reason enough, especially in matters of the heart) or wants to stop someone else from having or doing it. An **obstacle** arises when something prevents the motive from being satisfied— whether the obstacle is internal to the character (such as a moral dilemma or a rush of fear) or external (such as a character with a rival motive, or a storm at sea). A **consequence** follows when the satisfaction or frustration of that motive causes something important to happen, either resolving the first motive or setting another in motion.

A bridge blowing up is not, in itself, a dramatic action. But if someone wants to blow up the bridge to stop the advance of an enemy troop train, is almost prevented by a rival soldier, and finally succeeds, thus saving his country, now *that* explosion is dramatic in every sense of the word.

When a motive meets an obstacle, it usually doesn't just roll over and play dead; instead, it typically creates a **strategy** to try to find a way around the obstacle. It may be helpful to visualize the **life of an action** (which we can abbreviate "LOA") in graphic terms, using an example from Shakespeare's *Hamlet*.

Hamlet's revenge motive continues through a repeated pattern of obstacles and strategies until it reaches one of only two possible conclusions: **satisfaction** or **frustration**. The diagram in Figure 5.1 illustrates the initial steps in Hamlet's revenge. One interesting result of creating an LOA diagram for this character is that it tends to refute the oft-stated notion of Hamlet's passivity and indecision!

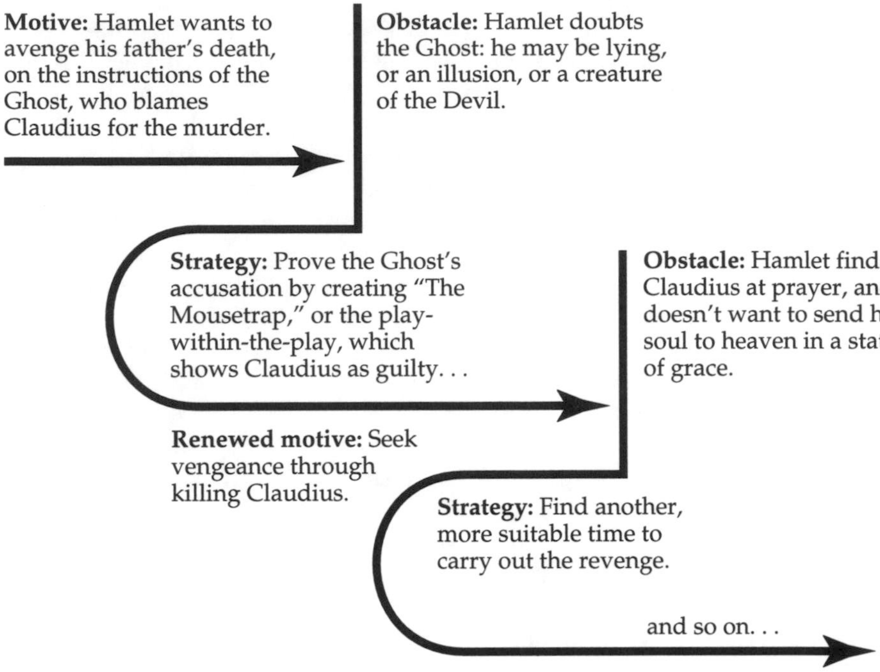

Motive: Hamlet wants to avenge his father's death, on the instructions of the Ghost, who blames Claudius for the murder.

Obstacle: Hamlet doubts the Ghost: he may be lying, or an illusion, or a creature of the Devil.

Strategy: Prove the Ghost's accusation by creating "The Mousetrap," or the play-within-the-play, which shows Claudius as guilty. . .

Obstacle: Hamlet finds Claudius at prayer, and doesn't want to send his soul to heaven in a state of grace.

Renewed motive: Seek vengeance through killing Claudius.

Strategy: Find another, more suitable time to carry out the revenge.

and so on. . .

FIGURE 5.1   Life-of-an-Action (LOA) Diagram for a Portion of Hamlet's Revenge Motive

Using the LOA Diagram

Some writers—especially those preparing functional analyses as actors and directors—may find it helpful to use LOA diagrams in detail, filling in significant motives, obstacles, and strategies for all the major characters in the play, while others may prefer to keep the image of the diagram in mind as a template for organizing their analysis. Either way, thinking specifically about the life of the action will ensure that the dramatic text comes to life as a sequence of **purposeful events** and that the essential **forward motion** of the theatrical experience is taken into account.

The Performing Texts: Verbal and Visual

In addition to their reliance on dramatic action as opposed to narrative and description, plays distinguish themselves from other literary forms by being **performing texts.** A play (both on the page and in production) communicates by means of two separate but deeply related systems of meaning, which might be called the **verbal** and **visual texts.**

The verbal text of a play comprises the **dialogue** spoken by the characters. The visual text consists of the **real or imaginary production elements** that the playwright suggests, either explicitly in stage directions or implicitly through references in the dialogue.

Exploring the Verbal Text

The verbal text is the primary resource for answers to important questions such as the following, which offer a way into the dramatic life of the play:

- What is the play's **main action?** What is accomplished, within the world of the play, by the events of the play? In other words, toward what state of affairs (changed or unchanged) does the play's action lead?
- What information does the dialogue contain about the **characters,** specifically their wants and needs? Their hopes and fears?
- What **contradictions** are apparent between how characters speak of themselves and how others speak about them?
- How much of the **characters' past** is revealed in the present-tense action of the play? How much is alluded to? How much is hidden?
- How do the characters respond to the **world around them?** Is it hostile? Supportive? Neutral?

Stating the Action through Dialogue

Actors often phrase dramatic actions for characters using strong, active, infinitive verbs; Hamlet's main action is "*to avenge* his father's death." This technique is equally apt for stating the main action of an entire play (also known to students of Stanislavsky as a "superobjective," or in the vocabulary of director and critic Harold Clurman, the "spine"). Thus, some possible statements: *Hamlet's* action is *to heal* what's "rotten in the state of Denmark." Ibsen's *A Doll House* seeks *to topple* the existing, oppressive state of marriage in search of a true union. In Williams's *Cat on a Hot Tin Roof*, the main action might be *to force* the truth to light, *to dispel* "the odor of mendacity."

Such statements allow the play analyst to keep sight of the dramatic engine of a text—the larger sense of where the play is going—even while examining details of language, image, and character. Directors and designers often find it useful to hold the main action as a benchmark against which to measure their production decisions: Does a given staging choice contribute to the realization of the main action? By using the LOA template, asking the basic questions listed under Exploring the Verbal Text, and thinking in strong verbs, the analyst can arrive at a highly specific understanding of the core dramatic values of a play.

The Author's Hand: Imagery and Metaphor

The verbal text is also the place to look for writerly devices such as repeated patterns of **imagery** and **metaphor;** we suggest your using the techniques of note taking, especially annotation of the text, described in Chapter 2, to highlight and analyze the images and metaphors in the play texts you study. A reader of Shakespeare's *A Midsummer Night's Dream*, for example, might be struck even on a first reading by the number of times the moon is mentioned; subsequent rereadings, with pencil (or other note-taking instrument) in hand, would yield a long list of lunar references, beginning with the very first speech:

> *Theseus:* Now, fair Hippolyta, our nuptial hour
>   Draws on apace. Four happy days bring in
>   Another *moon;* but O, methinks, how slow
>   This old *moon* wanes! She lingers my desires,
>   Like to a step-dame, or a dowager,
>   Long withering out a young man's revenue.
>
> *Hippolyta:* Four days will quickly steep themselves in night;
>   Four nights will quickly dream away the time;
>   And then the *moon*, like to a silver bow
>   New bent in heaven, shall behold the night
>   Of our solemnities.
>   (Act I, sc. 1; 11.1–11)

Not only does Shakespeare have each character invoke the moon directly, but each also indulges in a lunar **simile** as well (like to a *step-dame*, like to a *silver bow*), making the moon the major subject of the play's opening. The very next scene features four more references to the moon, in several different dramatic contexts. And so it goes throughout the play; the careful annotator will soon fill the play's margins (or a notebook) with lunar imagery both direct and implied.

Clearly Shakespeare is up to something here; the writer of a *literary analysis* might develop the theme as the basis for an essay on a system of verbal imagery that pervades the play, while the author of a *functional analysis* might make notes about the moon's relationship to madness (as a tool for the actors) or how it might come to serve as the central metaphor for the play (which could have a profound impact on the set and lighting designers). Both writers will have noticed the same feature of the verbal text, but they will put that information to different uses depending on their specific interests and the needs of their readers. (Shakespeare, meanwhile, being the crafty theatre professional that he is, is also making sure that his audience—outdoors, in the daylight—knows what time it is in the world of his play.)

"Hearing" the Verbal Text

Dialogue, of course, is written to be spoken, and this simple fact has several implications that the play analyst must bear in mind. First (and obviously), the audience in the theatre is **hearing** the play rather than **reading** it, and playwrights never forget that simple fact even if scholars sometimes do. There's a reason that Shakespeare uses *moon* so many times in the first five minutes of his play—he wants to make sure that we, in the listening and watching (and, in Elizabethan times, noisy) audience don't miss the importance of that image. Second, dialogue contains a number of values, beyond the surface meaning of the words, that a skillful actor (or a good reader) brings to life. To get at some of these implicit values, the following questions may be helpful:

- Are the characters saying what they mean, or is there a discernible **subtext**—the "between-the-lines" intention that is often different from or contradictory to what is actually said?
- What is the **tempo** of the dialogue? In musical terms, are the characters racing along at an *allegro* pace or are they walking through their dialogue at a leisurely *andante?* What does the tempo say about the emotional or intellectual temperature of the scene?
- Does the **rhythm** of the language suggest anything about the characters and the world of the play? In Shakespeare, rhythm is obviously an important factor, as he shifts from **verse** to **prose** and back again and as the verse itself changes depending on the emotional state of the character speaking. But prose dramatists also use rhythm as an expressive tool. Sentences may be *terse* and *clipped*, or *long* and *flowing*. Characters change their rhythms in response to the needs of the action in a given moment; consciously or unconsciously, they speak in the way that will help them get what they want. Listen to the flow of the language, full of melody and metaphor, in August Wilson's *The Piano Lesson* as Berniece tells her brother that he cannot sell their family's piano. The rhythm is every bit as evocative as the content of the words themselves, and leaves no doubt as to her meaning:

> *Berniece:* You ain't taking that piano out of my house. Look at this piano. Look at it. Mama Ola polished this piano with her tears for seventeen years. For seventeen years she rubbed on it till her hands bled. Then she rubbed the blood in . . . mixed it up with the rest of the blood on it. Every day that God breathed life into her body she rubbed and cleaned and polished and prayed over it.
>
> (Act I, scene 2)

- Does the playwright use **rhetorical devices** to give us clues about character or theme? Something of how a character's mind works is revealed by the way he or she places the **operative words**—the most important words and ideas in a sentence or speech. George Bernard Shaw's characters often use a verbal device called **contrast emphasis**—balancing one operative word (or phrase) against another to intensify the structure of their arguments—as in this example from *Major Barbara*. Here Andrew Undershaft makes a ringing speech about the political power he holds as an arms manufacturer (italics added to show operative words):

Undershaft: [*with a touch of brutality*] The *government* of your *country*! *I* am the government of your country: *I*, and *Lazarus*. Do you suppose that *you* and a half a dozen *amateurs* like you, sitting in a row in that foolish *gabble shop* [i.e., Parliament], can govern *Undershaft and Lazarus*? No, my friend: *you* will do what pays *us*. You will *make war* when it suits us, and *keep peace* when it doesn't. *You* will *find out* that *trade requires* certain measures when *we* have *decided* on those measures. When *I want* anything to keep my dividends *up*, *you* will discover that *my want* is a *national need*. When *other people* want something to keep my dividends *down*, *you* will call out the police and military. And in return *you* shall have the *support* and *applause* of *my* newspapers, and the *delight* of *imagining* that you are a *great statesman*. Government of your country! Be off with you, my boy, and *play* with your *caucuses* and *leading articles* and *historic parties* and *great leaders* and *burning questions* and the rest of your *toys*. *I* am going back to my *counting-house* to *pay the piper* and *call the tune*.
(Act III, scene 1)

• Are there moments where the lines overlap? In this example from Caryl Churchill's *Top Girls*, the playwright marks interrupted lines with the slash mark (/); the next character to speak begins at the slash mark in the previous character's line. This technique creates a very carefully orchestrated tumble of language; to understand both the music and meaning of the scene, it is crucial to hear the dialogue in the overlapping fashion that Churchill intends:

Marlene: I don't think religious beliefs are something we have in common. Activity yes.

Nijo: My head was active. / My head ached.

Joan: It's no good being active in heresy.

Isabella: What heresy? She's calling the Church of England / a heresy.

Joan: There are some very attractive / heresies.

Nijo: I had never heard of Christianity. Never / heard of it. Barbarians.

Marlene: Well I'm not a Christian. / And I'm not a Buddhist.

Isabella: You have heard of it?

(Act I, scene 1)

There are many ways in which a good play reader takes the performing flavor of the language into account in constructing a play analysis; the main point is to consider the verbal text as **speech in action** rather than as words on a page. Imagine yourself into the world of the play using the action, imagery, rhythm, structure, and flow of the dialogue as one of your primary tools. The playwright's visual text will be your other.

The Two Components of the Visual Text
The visual text of a play has both explicit and implicit components. Shakespeare—along with most playwrights working before **realistic scenery** became the norm in the late nineteenth century—says next to nothing about how the stage is to appear, instead relying on the dialogue to convey whatever information is necessary about visual matters. In more contemporary plays, the writer may describe the play's **imagined setting** in great detail, almost as a poet or novelist might see the scene (cf. the first page of a play by Tennessee Williams). Modern playwrights also may indicate lighting and costume ideas throughout the course of the play. These notations of the way the playwright sees the physical world of the play form the **explicit visual text.**

Directors and designers often use these suggestions as a point of departure rather than following them literally, and many contemporary playwrights offer such suggestions in an advisory spirit; on the other hand, Samuel Beckett was famous for insisting that the spare but precise descriptions of his explicit visual text be treated with the same respect as his dialogue.

The **implicit visual text** is a product of the play's action as imagined by the director, actors, and designers in the case of a produced play, or by the reader in the absence of a production. Dialogue reveals dramatic action, which in turn may suggest environment and movement; the level of tension in a given scene might determine how close the characters stand to one another; practical necessities create certain movement patterns while emotional ups and downs suggest others.

For example, when a character in A. R. Gurney's contemporary comedy *The Cocktail Hour* offers someone a drink, a stroll to the bar is imminent, even in the absence of a stage direction to that effect; the information is in the dialogue. When the Doctor takes Blanche DuBois offstage near the end of *A Streetcar Named Desire*, the rhythm and texture of their walk is evoked in Blanche's haunting line, "I have always depended on the kindness of strangers." On a more cosmic stage, King Lear's storm speech ("Blow, winds, and crack your cheeks, rage, blow . . . ") certainly offers a powerful suggestion about the accompanying visual text. Shakespeare has provided an implicit visual text through the language ("Spit, fire; spout, rain!") while leaving the explicit manifestation to the interpretive decisions of the reader/writer/producer.

STRUCTURE AND WORLD VIEW

The concept of **structure** is a way of talking about the playwright's fundamental assumptions about dramatic design—the rules that govern the imaginary world created by this writer for this play. A play's structure is visible in the way the playwright chooses (or refuses) to link the dramatic actions that make up the plot. Put another way, if the LOA diagram is the microscopic view of a play's building blocks, structure allows us to zoom out to the macroscopic perspective, to see the building as a whole.

The structure of a play is often the most telling clue about the author's world view for that play, and upon closer examination it's not difficult to see why this should be so. Playwrights set actions in motion through their characters and decide which of those actions we will see, in what order, and to what effect. Playwrights deal out rewards and punishments to their characters, leave their dramatic worlds in harmony or disarray, offer their characters (and audience) solace or uncertainty. In short, they function as a kind of deity within the world of their own creation.

If a playwright chooses a world in which actions have logical consequences and the story proceeds in a linear fashion with a beginning, middle, and ending that satisfies both the characters' and the audience's sense of **logical causality** (as in a great deal of pre-twentieth century drama), we might make certain inferences about that world as one possessing a reassuring order, with a governing intelligence overseeing the affairs of humankind.

If, on the other hand, the structure of the play is **nonlinear** and **discontinuous,** with characters acting outside logical motives and consequences (as in much contemporary drama), we might make entirely different inferences. This world may suggest to us the absence of a moral order, a controlling intelligence run amok or gone away, or (alternatively) a world free of the constraints of conventional societal structures.

Changes in Dramatic Structure through History

It is no accident that dramatic structure changes over the centuries in response to changing assumptions about theology, science, politics, gender, race, and other fundamental societal matters. Large world events can also trigger changes in world view and, therefore, structure; compare European drama before and after World War I (e.g., Henrik Ibsen versus Bertolt Brecht) for perhaps the starkest example of an abrupt shift from a logical, "well-made" world to one of brutal illogic and uncertain, shifting, nonlinear structures. In either case, the playwright offers us, through the choice of a dramatic structure, a world view that invites comparison with our own and provides the writer of a play analysis with fertile ground for interpretive work.

Keeping in mind the irony of Miss Prism's elegant definition of poetic justice in Oscar Wilde's *The Importance of Being Earnest*—"The good ended happily and the bad unhappily; that is what Fiction means"—we can also look to **outcomes** for certain insights into a play's dramatic design. Shakespeare offers us a range of plays, spanning all genres, in which kingdoms and families (dramatic worlds) are torn asunder by violence, ambition, bad leadership, romantic rivalries, and other causes, only to be healed at the end by the emergence of a new, positive force. Sometimes it's not a simplistic or frivolous question to ask, "Who's left standing at the end?" in order to get some sense of the playwright's world view—recognizing that the *who* might also be a *what*—a system of belief, a moral principle, a kingdom.

Themes and Meanings, or What's It All About?

You may have noticed that we have carefully avoided using the words **theme** and **meaning** until now. These words can be a trap for the unwary, since they tend to impose a static statement of value on a dynamic art form. And yet it is impossible to maintain that the concepts of theme and meaning have no application to plays and performances; artists usually do strive to create meanings and often operate with a sense of theme as a unifying, guiding principle. It is vitally important in analyzing drama, therefore, to think through the play's dramatic action step by step, consider the performing aspects of the verbal and visual texts, and look at the play's overall structure or dramatic design before attempting what is often the desired result of play analysis: an investigation of a play's themes and meanings.

The writer of a *functional analysis* might never need to settle on one final statement of theme or meaning; the form might be best understood as a method for getting the range of possibilities on the table so that the interpretive work of production can proceed. Some productions actively seek to underscore a certain **thematic value,** while others just as deliberately leave the question open. No matter what the aims of a particular production, it is important to remember that in the theatre, **meaning** is a *collaborative creation among artists, text, and audience, subject to subtle nightly revisions.* As any actor will confirm, a play that's uproariously funny on Wednesday night can be a serious drama on Thursday.

Literary analysis, on the other hand, might properly seek some sort of **thematic summation** of a play. The best way to guide your search for a statement of theme that's accurate and original is to interrogate yourself (and your notes) after finishing the play analysis tasks suggested. Ask yourself:

What is this play about? What kind of experience did the author want me to have? What am I left thinking about after it's over?

These are direct, honest routes into the heart of the matter.

Your dummy draft answers to these questions most likely will, when refined and supported with details from the play itself, lead you to an elegant statement of the play's theme as it has revealed itself to you. You might want to review some of the suggestions for the drafting and revising process in Chapter 3.

WRITING THE PLAY ANALYSIS: A CHECKLIST

No matter what kind of play analysis you are setting out to write, considering the following questions may help in getting started:

- Is the assignment to do a **functional** or a **literary** analysis?
- Who is the intended **audience?** (For a *functional analysis,* the writer alone, production collaborators, others? For a *literary analysis,* the reader of a critical introduction, a scholarly journal, a textbook, a professor?)
- What are the **principal dramatic actions** of the play? of the major characters? (Use the LOA diagram in Figure 5.1 to identify the course of specific major actions.)
- What observations can be made about the **verbal** and **visual texts** of the play?
- What is the **structure** of the play, and how does it reflect the playwright's **world view?**

- What are the **outcomes** for the principal characters, and do these outcomes offer any insight into the play's world view?
- What can be said about a **central theme** or **meaning** (or set of possible meanings) for the play?

In the dummy draft stage, try to develop responses to each of these points, in proportions appropriate to the type of paper and its intended audience. In so doing, you will have created an enormous cache of raw materials from which to shape almost any kind of play analysis.

FORMATS

Format of the Functional Analysis

A finished *functional analysis* may take the form of a cleaned-up, outlined, and bulleted version of your dummy draft; remember that at the outset of this chapter we referred to the functional analysis as a set of notes. It's not meant for publication; it is rather a tool for communicating your understanding of how a play *works* to those who need to know. It should be legible and well written, but it does not need to follow the formal conventions of the academic paper. Actors, directors, designers, and dramaturgs may each tailor the form of the functional analysis so that it yields the information most relevant to their particular pursuit.

Format of the Literary Analysis

A *literary analysis*, by contrast, should follow the more traditional term paper format, paying close attention to matters of style and mechanics. In this case, the dummy draft should go through the full rough draft/revision process described in Chapter 3. For formatting purposes, pay particular attention to the Formatting section in that chapter.

The important point, no matter which kind of play analysis you are writing, is to grapple with the dramatic text as a living, action-based document equipped with an enormous amount of information—both verbal and visual—that can only be recovered by imagining the play as a blueprint for performance.

Sample Excerpts: Functional and Literary Analyses

The following are excerpts from analyses of *A Midsummer Night's Dream*. These brief excerpts are presented by way of illustrating the differences in format and style between the two kinds of writing, not to suggest a complete or definitive interpretation of the play.

Functional Analysis

- *Assignment:* As director of an upcoming production of *A Midsummer Night's Dream,* analyze the play's action and imagery in a set of notes. Begin to develop ideas about a possible central metaphor for your production based on the text.
- *Intended audience:* Your creative colleagues—the set, lighting, sound, and costume designers; the dramaturg; and rehearsal notes for yourself to pass along to the actors when appropriate.

Sample Excerpt

1. **Main Action:** *To bring true lovers together* by resolving the conflicts that are keeping them apart—those same conflicts that are keeping the entire world of the play off balance, because neither the human (mortal) characters nor the fairies (representing the spirit world? the unconscious?) are at peace. Another, larger view of the main action might be *to heal the rift in the world.* A world out of tune is brought into harmony. Perhaps we can reflect this in the progression of our sound and musical choices as well.

   - Every relationship and plot line somehow has to do with conflicted love, and all are resolved happily, except the pseudotragic story of Pyramus and Thisbe that comprises the play-within-the-play performed by the "rude mechanicals."
   - The **obstacles** to these actions of healing and resolution are generated by two things: (1) the inherent inability (in either kingdom, mortal or fairy) to get love right in the first place (Theseus wooed Hippolyta with his sword, Egeus stands in Lysander and Hermia's way, Oberon and Titania are fighting over possession of a "changeling boy" who is really a war prize); and (2) the fairies' clumsy attempts to engineer a solution.
   - Oberon's desire to set things right is strong enough to ensure that new strategies are always ready when the first ones fail. He finally succeeds in creating the "proper" matchups. The **consequences** of failure are severe: continued discord in both the mortal and fairy worlds (floods, famines, wars, etc.).

2. **The Text:** The language seems to have a high number of **regular iambic pentameter** lines, so that when the basic rhythm is varied (such as in Egeus's first line, "Full of vexation come I, with complaint . . . " which is agitated and goes against the iambic flow, being almost dactylic) it is clearly purposeful.

   - Also a large number of *rhymed* lines, suggesting perhaps a fairy-tale or mythic quality.

- Several *songs* (sung by the fairies, e.g., "You spotted snakes with double tongue . . . ")
- Other passages of *spells and benedictions,* such as the fairies' blessing of Theseus's palace in a very lyrical tetrameter, or four-beat line, e.g., "Through the house give glimmering light, / By the dead and drowsy fire . . . ")
- And, in a *comic vein,* the play-within-the-play, which is set in a variety of meters from an old-fashioned, bombastic pentameter ("O grim-look'd night! O night with hue so black!") to a sing-songy doggerel with only two or three beats in the line ("But stay! O spite! / But mark, poor knight, / What dreadful dole is here!").
- The overall effect of the language is highly **flexible, musical,** and finally **magical.** Let's find a production style to match!

3. **The Moon:** If there's a key word in this text, and one which might help us toward a central metaphor, *moon* is it (along with *dream,* but that's a subject for later). The first scene (Theseus and Hippolyta discussing their impending marriage) is all about the moon, with three direct uses in eleven lines, and two extended similes based on the moon. Then, immediately, Egeus comes in, accusing Lysander of courting Hermia "by *moonlight* at her window" in defiance of her engagement to Demetrius. Theseus tells her to obey her father's will or be prepared to become a nun, "Chanting faint hymns to the cold fruitless *moon.*" Almost every scene has one or more significant lunar references.

- The moon is the light by which all the mischief, mistakes, jealousies, and strife take place. Oberon sees his counterpart for the first time in the play (Act II) and greets her with this: "Ill met by *moonlight,* proud Titania."
- The moon's power to confuse is only broken by the approach of dawn, as the lovers awake and the fairies, now harmonious, retire (as Oberon says, "Swifter than the wand'ring moon" [Act IV]).
- When moonlight returns, it is harmlessly and comically personified by Starveling the tailor as "Moonshine" in the mechanicals' play (Act V); it has lost its power to hurt.
- Let's all think about the connotations and resonances of the moon as a metaphor—madness, the tides, time itself, etc.—and how it might affect both the design and the performance of our production.

From here, the author of the functional analysis will go on to discuss other **key elements** in the verbal and visual texts (already noted as a subject for more exploration is the word *dream,* and there are other significant patterns of language and image as well); the play's **structure** and **world view;** and might conclude with some thoughts about a central **theme** for the production, perhaps expressed in a **metaphor** (e.g., "moon" or "dream" in this example) that every member of the creative team can use as a touchstone for his or her work.

This set of notes that we call a functional analysis might also serve as the predrafting stage, or even the dummy draft, of a more connected inquiry into a specific aspect of the play that could become a literary analysis. The following several paragraphs may help to illustrate this process.

Literary Analysis

- *Assignment:* Write a paper analyzing some aspect of *A Midsummer Night's Dream.* Suggested areas of investigation include language, theme, characters, and/or structure. Base your analysis firmly on the text of the play.
- *Intended audience:* The professor and students in a dramatic literature course. You may wish to imagine a secondary audience, such as the readers of an edition of the play for which you are writing the introduction.

Sample Excerpt

"Find Out Moonshine, Find Out Moonshine":
Lunar Images in A Midsummer Night's Dream

With this urgent plea to "look in the almanac" for the lunar calendar in Act III, scene 1 of Shakespeare's *A Midsummer Night's Dream,* Bottom the Weaver unwittingly underscores the importance of moonshine—indeed, of all things lunar—in the system of imagery that runs through the play. The moon functions, in a sense, as a presiding spirit over the action, providing the light by which all the mischief, mistakes, jealousies, and strife take place.

The first scene, in which Theseus and Hippolyta discuss their impending marriage, introduces the moon as a key verbal image and as a keeper of time (by extension, perhaps, of destiny as well), with three direct uses and two similes based on the moon:

Theseus: Now, fair Hippolyta, our nuptial hour
    Draws on apace. Four happy days bring in
    Another *moon;* but O, methinks, how slow
    This old *moon* wanes! She lingers my desires,
    Like to a step-dame, or a dowager,
    Long withering out a young man's revenue.

Hippolyta: Four days will quickly steep themselves in night;
    Four nights will quickly dream away the time;

And then the *moon*, like to a silver bow
New bent in heaven, shall behold the night
Of our solemnities.
> (1.1.1–11; emphasis added)

Theseus and Hippolyta use the moon as a rhetorical device to conceal their discomfort; we learn a few lines later that Theseus has abducted his bride-to-be: "Hippolyta, I woo'd thee with my sword, / And won thy love doing thee injuries" (1.1.16–17). Citing the slowness of the waning moon, Theseus expresses his impatience to be married. Hippolyta's response, which seems to say, "What's the rush?" invokes an image of the moon as the virgin goddess, Diana, the chaste huntress with her "silver bow"—probably not the kind of "solemnities" that Theseus has in mind.

Soon after, old Egeus comes in, accusing Lysander of courting Hermia "by *moonlight* at her window" (1.1.30) in defiance of her engagement to Demetrius. Theseus tells her to obey her father's will or be prepared to become a nun, "Chanting faint hymns to the cold fruitless *moon*" (1.1.73).

In the first scene of the play, then, the moon has been associated with both romance and romantic discord, with a problematic marriage and a problematic engagement. In the next act, the moon will take on an even more disturbing glow, as it presides over the warfare in the fairy world.

When the fairy king Oberon sees his counterpart for the first time, he greets her thus: "Ill met by *moonlight*, proud Titania" (2.1.60). Titania's response to his accusations of betrayal is a powerful catalogue of the evils visited upon the mortal world by the strife between the fairy King and Queen, including this significant lunar reference: "Therefore the *moon* (the governess of floods,) / Pale in her anger, washes all the air, / That rheumatic diseases do abound" (2.1.103–105).

Throughout the course of the action, the moon exerts a complex and frequently disturbing influence on the world of the play, providing a source of light that permeates the imagination of both character and spectator.

Observe how the writer of this paper has followed the traditional structure of the academic paper of literary analysis. The paper begins with the **thesis paragraph,** in which the idea that the paper will demonstrate is clearly stated: "The moon functions in a sense as a presiding spirit over the action. . . ." This paragraph leads the reader to assume that the subsequent paragraphs will argue convincingly how the play, both the verbal and visual texts, supports this "presiding" role of the moon.

Beyond the excerpt we have included, the writer of this literary analysis will likely go on to enumerate the additional significant references to the moon, showing how their use relates to the entire system of lunar imagery in the play. Since the play's action has been described as the "healing of a rift in the world" (in notes taken for the dummy draft and the functional analysis), the essay will probably conclude with an examination of how the moon's baneful influences are redeemed, or at least negated, by the home-spun comical moon of the play-within-the-play staged by Bottom the Weaver and his colleagues. This point will also provide a structural reintegration of the opening paragraph of the paper, with its reference to the rehearsal of the "rude mechanicals" and its call to "find out moonshine."

A FINAL WORD ON FINAL WORDS: CRAFTING A STRONG CONCLUSION

Good essays have a sense of structure just as good plays do, and returning to the opening theme of a paper is often a satisfying way to craft a conclusion. Be wary, however, of the mere restatement of your introduction dressed up as a conclusion. Too many papers begin "As this paper will show . . ." and conclude with "As this paper has shown. . . ." Reintegration of an opening theme is a more organic process, which occurs as a result of an overall structural idea for the paper.

6

THEATRE HISTORY

The history of the theatre in any given place and time opens a window on a surprisingly wide world. The plays that a certain city chooses to watch, the way they're written and performed, how the actors are paid, what the playhouses look like—these "theatre history" questions lead inevitably to other histories, such as those of literature, politics, economics, art and architecture, sociology, and culture.

THE THEATRICAL LENS

Drama provides an unusually honest record of a society's preoccupations, hopes, and fears because it offers its community a chance to look at itself in action; and though we called it a window above and Hamlet proposes that the true purpose of playing is "to hold, as 'twere, a mirror up to nature," the optical instrument that perhaps most accurately describes the function of drama in society is the *lens*. Theatre, like a lens, focuses our attention selectively; it magnifies and reduces, sometimes inverts and distorts, but always points us toward a new and carefully constructed image of the world at which it is aimed.

The theatre historian uses the lens to look more closely at the ways in which the world shapes the theatre and vice versa. For one historian, the image in the lens's eye might be the audience; for another, the union of the playwright's art with that of the actors and designers, under the influence of the politics and economics of their place and time. Still another might turn the lens on the way theatre buildings are designed and constructed in response to changing cultural imperatives, seeking reasons why theatres alternately grow and shrink, change shape, move indoors and out, become ostentatiously ornate or severely simple, reflecting alterations in artistic thinking and public desire. The lens might focus on the way assumptions about actors and acting change; women finally take the stage in Restoration England, styles of performance pursue an ever-shifting notion of "realism" (or avoid it altogether), and the social acceptability of actors varies from near-ostracism to celebrity worship. All of these subjects and more are available to the gaze of the theatrical lens.

The theatre historian's task, then, is to choose where to focus the lens. This question, like so many others in writing about theatre, finally resolves itself around identifying the **intended audience** and the **scope** and **purpose** of the work.

Theatre history typically gets written in one of three forms: the **overview** or **survey** (e.g., Oscar Brockett's *History of the Theatre*, now in its eighth edition, and a standard text in many college courses); the **book-length study of a specific topic** in theatre history (e.g., Gerald Bordman's *American Musical Theatre: A Chronicle*); and the **article** or **monograph**, which would appear in a scholarly journal such as *Theater History Studies* or *Theatre Journal*.

TYPES OF THEATRE HISTORY

There are many ways to break down the field of theatre history into smaller, more manageable units. The following is only one *schema*, but it is helpful because it allows the writer to begin focusing the research and writing task from the beginning, without predetermining the outcome or unduly restricting the breadth of reading that goes into any successful theatre history project. You might consider that the history of theatre (as distinct from the history of drama, which is more concerned with the literary values of the texts themselves) can be divided into three basic areas of inquiry: the **physical theatre**, the **social theatre**, and the **performing theatre**.

The Physical Theatre

Writing in this category invites the exploration of the development of:

- *theatre architecture*, including how and where theatres are constructed
- the theatre's *size and shape* relative to the population and its theatre-going habits
- the *technical capabilities* of the playhouse (trap doors? painted flats? computerized lighting systems?) and how they serve and influence the playwriting traditions of the time

- the purpose and style of the *scenery, costumes, and lighting* (why do some periods seem to depend heavily on design elements while others seem to ignore them?)

Much can be learned about the role of theatre within a given society by examining the playhouses themselves. For example, a research project might compare the huge, outdoor public theatres of the Hellenic period with the small, indoor, court theatres of the European Renaissance. A theatre historian might be able to ask certain questions about the nature of public life in the two eras, and theatre's role within it. Alternatively, the physical comparisons might lead directly to an examination of the different types of plays performed in each kind of playhouse, and whether the capabilities of the theatres shaped the writing of the plays, or the plays demanded certain capabilities of the theatres.

The location of theatres can offer additional insight into their role in a society. In Shakespeare's London, for example, no public theatres were allowed within the city limits; the Globe and its rivals were located across the Thames, on the South Bank, in a somewhat disreputable neighborhood where the competition included arenas for bear baiting. In New York City in the 1990s, theatres are being reclaimed for legitimate use in the heart of Times Square, spearheading the revival of an area once renowned as a hub of illicit activity and debased "entertainments" both live and filmed. The examination of the sociological and economic trends behind these facts might be an exciting focus for the theatre historian's research.

The physical theatre is also tied inextricably to the **progress of technology.** Almost as soon as discoveries are made, the theatre attempts to incorporate them into stage practices. There has been no greater revolution in the technology of theatre, for example, than the introduction of electric lighting. Its presence made theatres instantly safer, as the risk of fire from gaslight and oil lamps fell away. On the artistic side of the ledger, electric lamps placed in spotlights allowed early twentieth-century directors and designers to reveal and conceal areas of the stage precisely, with light alone, for the first time in the more than two thousand-year history of the theatre.

The implications of that seemingly simple act are still being explored, as lighting has come under sophisticated computer control. It is possible to claim, for instance, that the late 20th century megamusical (e.g, *The Phantom of the Opera, Cats*) would not have come into being as it did without the introduction of computerized control not only of lighting but of stage machinery. Throughout time, the theatre historian can trace the changing relationship between technology and dramaturgy.

A closely similar relationship exists between **dramaturgy** and **the practice of design.** Scenery, costumes, and lighting have evolved in response not only to technology but to changing ideas about the very essence of the theatrical event.

When we go to the theatre, are we looking for an image of the lives we lead? If so, we are likely to find realistic sets and costumes there. Or are we interested in mythic stories, larger-than-life passions, and poetry? In that case, we will probably see scenery and clothing that operates on a more metaphorical level, or in a highly conventionalized way (as in the limited but suggestive use of design that we associate with the Greeks or Shakespeare's theatre).

Lighting responds in similar ways to the changing aesthetics of theatre, sometimes offering almost subliminal support of mood and atmosphere, and at other times creating self-consciously theatrical effects. Each design element, considered separately or together, can offer the theatre historian a wealth of insight into the theatrical practices and aesthetic assumptions of a given time and place.

The Social Theatre

A writer interested in the broad category of theatre-in-society will be drawn to questions such as:

- Who goes to the theatre?
- Why do they go?
- How many go, and how often?
- How much do they pay?
- How do they behave?

These issues might seem to be just as properly the province of students of sociology or business administration, but in fact they engage theatre historians in passionate inquiry. The nature of the audience has been a primary shaping force in drama and theatre throughout the life of the art form.

Just as theatre architecture changes in response to changing assumptions in a society, so too does the audience that fills (or fails to fill) the theatres. A theatre historian might take note, for example, of the mixing of social classes associated with Shakespeare's Globe Theatre, with its groundlings, aristocrats, and vendors of various goods and services all mingling, if not in the same precise location, at least within the walls of the theatre building. Was the audience for Greek tragedy, that most public spirited of all dramas, restricted to citizens of Athens, meaning men? If so, what does that say about Attic democracy? Why did theatre attendance swell so dramatically in European cities during the early 1800s, a period associated with sweeping economic changes, political turmoil, and urban squalor? A theatre historian might well take note of changes in an audience's demographic description—the quantifiable data about class, race, number, origin, and other factors—and do research in an attempt to find out the root causes of those changes.

An audience is a living partner in the production of a play, and theatre historians have always been interested in how audiences throughout history have chosen to play their role. Today, when we go to a live stage performance, we expect a certain code of conduct to be observed. Our customary (if blurry) separation between stage and audience is not fixed, however, and theatre history records many instances of audiences engaging in disruptive, even riotous activity in the theatre. In certain times and places, the atmosphere in the theatre has resembled the church; in others, the town square or bazaar. One of the most interesting tasks of the theatre historian is to discover which is the case in any given period, and why.

The Performing Theatre

One of the most interesting—and difficult—avenues for exploring theatre history is the changing nature of performance itself. Over the centuries, the core ideas of theatre's *essence* may have remained largely intact, but the way that they are put into *practice* has shifted repeatedly and significantly. The theatre historian might choose a particular period to study in great depth, collecting information on such questions as:

- *The state of the texts:* Were they played uncut, with some cuts, or with heavy adaptations?
- *The psychological assumptions of the time:* For starters, is the world in question pre- or post-Freudian?
- *The aspects of acting contemporary commentators talked about most enthusiastically:* Was it vocal prowess, emotional depth, physical skill, naturalness, or something else?
- *The prevailing theatrical styles:* For example, was the performance expected to create an illusion of reality?
- *What actors looked like in their roles:* Check contemporary paintings, engravings, book illustrations, and periodicals for hints about the actor's choice of costume, gesture, facial expression, and even lighting—but take all such renderings with a grain of salt, as the artist may have been expressing his or her own interpretation of the role as much as the actor's.

Before the advent of recording technology, especially film and video, the actor's art was notoriously hard to capture. It is possible to hear a scratchy recording of the great Sarah Bernhardt (one of the quintessential stars of the mid- to late nineteenth century) made toward the end of her career; but for the centuries of famous actors before her, the record is made up entirely of documents—reviews (which themselves became a serious endeavor only as recently as the eighteenth century), diaries, paintings and engravings, and references in literature.

The theatre historian, then, plays the role of an imaginative detective, putting together disparate pieces of evidence to create a "best-guess" idea of a particular style of performance. Imprecise as this procedure can be, it is nonetheless useful in helping shape an overall picture of theatrical production in a given place and time. Joined with more concrete information about the physical theatre and the playwriting of the moment, educated guesswork about acting styles can tell us much about the way theatre is made and received.

These questions can begin to lead the theatre historian to some conclusions about possible performance practices. If a recording is also available, it can obviously become an important resource; but theatre historians are aware that film and video are capable of almost limitless manipulations (and distortions) of sound and image, so that final conclusions about the original performance that lies behind the film are almost as risky as those based purely on historical documents.

The performing theatre is the category of theatre history that requires, perhaps, the most original and imaginative thought. The writer must be able to collate historical records, knowledge of the play and the period, and inspired assumptions into a plausible account of a slippery notion—an actor's style. But this kind of work is also among the most interesting in theatre history, for without it the great performances of the past would be mute.

RESEARCHING AND WRITING THE THEATRE HISTORY PAPER

Any worthwhile assignment in theatre history presumes at least two things:

- that the writer will engage in a significant research effort
- that this effort will feed the writing of a paper that treats the research materials in an original way

No one is interested in writing (or reading!) a paper that merely restates information already easily available in textbooks. The research phase of the work should, therefore, energize and inspire the writing rather than simply provide a collection of quotations and facts to be strung together with minimal connective tissue.

The Chicken or the Egg?

Energizing research occurs when several conditions are present; the most important of these is a *topic* that interests the writer. In the absence of prior knowledge and enthusiasm, though, how is the writer supposed to generate interest in a specific topic? Here we come to the chicken-and-egg question inherent in research: Which should come first, a carefully selected and limited research question, or the beginnings of the research itself?

Read First, Ask Questions Later

We advocate a "read first, ask questions later" approach to beginning your research. Quite possibly, the subject area will be at least partially defined to begin with. In a typical theatre history course, the professor will provide a range of questions, a list of topics, or some parameters such as periods, authors, or issues in theatre history. This gives the writer at least some direction in the initial research; but be careful not to settle on a specific research question too early. Read around the subject area first before selecting a topic and focusing your research more narrowly. As you read, consider keeping a reading response log (as described in Chapter 2) to record your ideas about the reading and help you focus your study.

For the sake of illustration, let's assume that you have an assignment to write a paper on some aspect of the history of stage design, within the period covered by a course in "History of the Theatre from 1600 to the Present." This topic falls within the category of the *physical theatre* outlined earlier.

A superficial survey of the subject *might* be squeezed into eight or ten pages, but the result would almost certainly not have room for original thought, analysis, or reference to anything outside the breathless recitation of facts. You're looking for a way to narrow the subject area without, at this early point, settling on a final topic.

Your reading for the course has probably included some plays along with the usual textbook materials of theatre history. You might begin focusing your research by **rereading some plays** that struck you as particularly interesting, and then exploring other works by the same author or by authors from the same period. This will fulfill one of the key principles of theatre history:

1. *Reading into the dramatic literature of the time makes all subsequent research more meaningful.*

After you've read some plays (and perhaps written about them in your log), you might begin to consider some avenues for more topic-centered research. Let us say, for example, that the play you use to launch your inquiry is Henrik Ibsen's *A Doll House* (published in 1879). Reading both forward (to *Ghosts*) and backward (to *Pillars of Society*), you notice the extraordinarily detailed set descriptions provided by Ibsen, and you start to wonder about his need to create such exacting instructions for the reader and producer, instructions that were notably absent from the previous plays you've read for the course. Your coursework has already given you some notion of the evolution of stage design over the course of the nineteenth century, from two-dimensional painted backdrops to three-dimensional, realism-based "box sets."

A Question Begins to Grow

You wonder: Could it be that Ibsen's stage directions are a part of that transition? Some questions may now start to develop themselves in your mind and take shape in your log: How did stage design make the leap from two-dimensional to three-dimensional scenery? Who were some of the artists responsible? Was it primarily the work of playwrights, directors, designers, or some combination of all three? Did Ibsen's changing sense of stage design influence his playwriting, or vice versa?

These questions comprise several possible research topics, but that is appropriate at this stage of your work. Keep several questions in mind as you begin researching, to allow for the possibility of unexpected discoveries—which brings us to a second principle of research:

   2. *Create the conditions under which "serendipity scholarship" can occur.*

The unplanned intersection of information and ideas can only happen when a question is broad enough to pull in material from many directions at once. A too-narrow question, settled on too early, leads inevitably to a predictable set of facts and is unlikely to provide you with an original combination of data.

The Hunt Begins

Now you're in the library, starting to gather your sources. At the online catalogue, you enter your search keywords. Remembering the principle of serendipity scholarship, you keep your search broad at this point. The keyword "Ibsen" will yield thousands of hits on an Internet search engine, and quite possibly hundreds in a large library collection. A more targeted search, such as "Ibsen+design+realism" will yield many fewer, which might seem to make the research task easier.

It will not. At this point, *more is more*. You should use this first approach to the library holdings (or Web-based resources) as a direction finder, not a bibliography. If you're lucky enough to be working at a library that still maintains an old-fashioned, extensively cross-referenced card catalogue, you might also consult it; card catalogues reflect the experiences and insights of generations of highly skilled librarians and may direct your attention to research leads that the computer search would miss.

In any case, with your long, flowing printout (or slips of handwritten call numbers) in hand, march boldly through the stacks, looking not only for the books the computer found—but for relevant material nearby that the search engine may have missed but which the librarians who shelved the books did not. This is our third principle of research:

3. *Browse the stacks; don't simply trust the catalogue.*

If a book in a certain area of the stacks proves useful, chances are there are several more in the immediate vicinity that will also contain items of interest. Take the time—it doesn't take long—to scan the table of contents, the index, some key chapter beginnings, to see if your "serendipity scholarship" engine is working that day. Not only will this searching add to the depth and originality of your research, but it is fun to do—and when you make discoveries this way, it can actually be a bit of a (shhh!) thrill.

Serendipity Strikes

Although you've been concentrating your research thus far on Ibsen's play texts and on books treating the history of stage design, your shelf browsing leads you to several fat volumes of Ibsen biography. In one of these, you come across Ibsen's youthful efforts as a watercolor painter. Soon you discover that he staged productions long before he reached renown as a playwright. You come across a photograph of one of his early staging diagrams from the 1850s, and you notice that the setting is very much of the two-dimensional, painted variety that Ibsen was later to reject in his detailed stage directions.

But something else catches your eye—a reference by a critic to one of Ibsen's productions in 1856 praises his abandonment of "the stiff and unnatural old-fashioned custom of running right down to the footlights or turning to the audience whenever they have anything to say . . . [they] turn to each other when conversing."[*]

---

[*]Michael Meyer, *Henrik Ibsen* (London: Rupert Hart-Davis, 1967), vol. 1, p. 126.

A Question Begins to Take Shape

The theatre historian's mind is now hard at work putting data together: stage conventions in the mid-nineteenth century were artificial and two dimensional; Ibsen's own work in the 1850s seemed to be trying to advance those conventions, and he had some ability as a visual artist/painter; twenty years later, as a respected playwright, he began to develop extraordinarily detailed and specific stage directions. These pieces of data, which might have remained separate in a more narrowly focused initial research effort, now lead you to some potentially interesting questions:

- What are the connections between Ibsen's early theatre work and his later insistence on a completely visualized physical environment for his plays?
- What led him to develop a more realistic style of production?
- How did his increasingly detailed stage environments affect the dramaturgy of his plays?

These questions are similar to the ones with which you began your search, but they are much more focused. You're now ready to do the kind of specific research that can only take place when you've narrowed your questions into a topic.

Questions Become a Topic

It can be helpful at this point in your writing process to try to craft a **title** for your paper—and then to focus your work from this point forward on **fulfilling the promise of your title.** It seems as if the majority of books and articles written in academic circles make use of the two-part title, or title and subtitle, separated by a colon. The main title is often a quotation or an imagistic reflection of the subject, while the subtitle (after the colon) is typically a more concrete, specific description of the topic. If you adopt this formula, your title might look something like this: "A World in Three Dimensions: The Growth of Realism in Ibsen's Stage Designs."

Now, with your narrowed research questions and your tentative paper title in mind, you are ready to complete your research and undertake the dummy drafting, rough drafting, and revision process described in Chapter 3 of this book.

A Word on Sources in Theatre History

If you use the research principles we've advocated here, you will have no trouble amassing a diverse and interesting **bibliography** in support of your theatre history paper. Be cautious, however, if your main sources are all *ter-*

tiary references. *Primary* and *secondary* sources are preferred, because they're in closer touch with the original subject matter.

- **Primary sources** are original documents such as letters, eyewitness accounts, diary entries, public records, photographs, drawings, and interviews. The text of a play can often be considered a primary source as well.
- **Secondary sources** include biographical studies, in which the biographer has consulted primary sources; scholarly books and articles on a specific field of theatre history (e.g., a book-length study of the origins of drama, an article in a journal on the theatre in Boston in colonial times); and other writings in which a scholar has served as mediator or interpreter between the original materials and the reader.
- **Tertiary sources** include general theatre history textbooks, which consult and compile all the kinds of sources just listed but may not contribute any original research or cross-checking.

An Internet caveat: While the Internet is a source of information without precedent in terms of *quantity*, the *quality* of much of that information is highly unreliable. A careful researcher will crosscheck facts derived from the Web. The writer of the theatre history paper that follows discovered several erroneous statements presented as fact on various sites.

Be sure to study Websites carefully to determine by whose authority the information has been entered or linked to the site. Personal Websites are notoriously unreliable. More reliable are official sites of universities and other authoritative research organizations. Nevertheless, the careful researcher always crosschecks information to the degree possible.

Some Ideas for Using Primary Sources

Primary sources are readily available for many contemporary subjects in theatre history, such as major Broadway and regional theatre productions and artists of the last half-century or so. If your subject matter takes you in that direction, you should find a wealth of journalistic material both in print and in the form of television interviews, documentaries, and even, occasionally, an archival videotape of significant productions. Two libraries, New York's Lincoln Center Library and Washington, D.C.'s Martin Luther King, Jr. Library, feature major collections of such videos.

Studying Your Own Community's Theatrical Life and History. A compelling research topic might be found in some aspect of theatrical life in your locality. Many cities and towns throughout the United States have rich and largely undocumented histories of theatre production by touring companies, community playhouses, and academic institutions. The theatrical traditions of larger cities are usually documented fairly well by the major newspapers, and many libraries hold (or can obtain) a microfiche record of newspapers stretching back decades; this information is slowly making its way online as well, and news archives are increasingly searchable on the Internet.

If you are writing about your own city or town's theatre history, you have the opportunity to do some first-hand primary research in the form of interviews—and by engaging in what we might call "tennis-shoe archaeology," visiting the sites of theatres past and present to see what remains of their architecture and what their location might suggest about the life of the community during the period of the theatre's existence. By undertaking this kind of theatre history you are not only learning about research and writing, but contributing new knowledge to the world's store. You might even consider publishing your results on the Internet or in a local newspaper or magazine.

SUMMARY: THE THREE MAIN PRINCIPLES

This chapter points the student writer toward a more active, engaged, and enjoyable way to take up the challenge of theatre history while at the same time increasing the scholarly value of the effort. Keep in mind our three helpful principles of theatre history research:

1. *Reading into the dramatic literature of the time makes all subsequent research more meaningful.*
2. *Create the conditions under which "serendipity scholarship" can occur.*
3. *Browse the stacks; don't simply trust the catalogue.*

Remember to start with a fairly broad research question, then develop more interesting, focused versions of the question based on your initial research. Take careful notes on your reading and use the reading response log to help focus your research and explore ideas. From there, create a topic and a title for your paper; and then begin to write.

We've noted elsewhere that probably 80 percent of the time spent on this kind of paper will be devoted to the research, including your predraft writing. If you proceed along the lines sketched out above, that time will be both intellectually alive and will greatly ease the ultimate task of writing the theatre history paper.

A SAMPLE THEATRE HISTORY PAPER

The following paper extends the process begun in the example given under Researching and Writing the Theatre History Paper to demonstrate how a writer might begin to flesh out the connections suggested by the initial questions. Sources are cited in the MLA style, using an abbreviated form, in parentheses, within the text of the paper; this is one good way of avoiding the use of footnotes or endnotes and it provides the reader with an easy reference to your "Works Cited" bibliography for the complete citation. Your professor (or publisher) may recommend other standard forms, and we also refer you to Chapter 8 in this book for further guidance on proper citation of sources using MLA standards.

A World in Three Dimensions:
The Growth of Realism in Ibsen's Stage Designs

In the 1850s, the man who was to become the author of such revolutionary plays as *A Doll House, Ghosts,* and *Hedda Gabler* was toiling as a stage director and designer in Bergen, fighting against the confining conventions of the theatre of his time. These included scenic designs that consisted largely of painted backdrops, with two-dimensional furniture painted right on the cloth; stage movement that restricted the actors to a formal semicircle and to stepping forward to say their lines; and a lack of specificity in scenery, costumes, or behavior (Brockett and Findlay, ch. 1).

But Henrik Ibsen, though his most important plays were still twenty to thirty years in the future, was already working toward the introduction of a more lifelike, natural, three-dimensional quality to the stage. Ibsen biographer Michael Meyer cites a review from Trondhejm, a town in northern Norway that Ibsen's company visited in 1856:

> It deserves to be remarked . . . that the actors have abandoned the stiff and unnatural old-fashioned custom of running right down to the footlights or turning to the audience whenever they have anything to say . . . the actors keep quite far upstage, and . . . turn to each other when conversing. (Meyer 1: 126)

Ibsen's attempt to break free from the confines of two-dimensional scenery had its roots in the daily work that the young playwright found himself engaged in. According to Prof. Bjørn Hemmer, this long apprenticeship in the professional theatre offered Ibsen exposure to a wide world of ideas:

> For eleven years the young Ibsen was occupied with day to day practical stagework, and it follows that he had to keep himself well informed about the latest contemporary European theatrical art. He worked with rehearsals of new plays and was . . . in close contact with the art of the stage for a long, uninterrupted period. . . . [H]e acquired a sharp eye for theatrical techniques and possibilities. (Hemmer 1)

continued

continued

Ibsen's decision to adopt a three-dimensional, realistic idea of stage design went hand in hand with his abandonment of verse, epic drama, and romantic or nationalistic themes, which had characterized his playwriting from 1850 through about 1875. The movement would not reach complete fruition until he began his cycle of prose dramas that begins with *Pillars of Society* in 1877 and concludes with his last work, *When We Dead Awaken,* 1899. An examination of the changes in Ibsen's published stage directions—the indications of scene that begin each of his plays—shows how his thinking became both more detailed and more three-dimensional over time.

In *Love's Comedy,* a rhymed-couplet romance written in 1862 and referred to by one scholar as Ibsen's "first assured masterpiece" (Johnston 104), the opening stage direction reads:

> The set represents a beautiful garden, irregularly but tastefully laid out; the fiord and the outlying islands can be seen in the background. To the left of the spectator is the main building, with a verandah and above it, an open window; to the right, in the foreground, an open summer-house with benches and a table. The scene is bathed in the vivid light of late afternoon. It is early summer; the fruit trees are in blossom. (*Love's Comedy* 99)

It is a romantically conceived setting, the vast majority of which could be (and would have been) realized in two-dimensional backdrops, wings, and overhead borders painted and cut out to represent foliage. It is, perhaps, significant that Ibsen uses the word "represents" in the first sentence of his stage direction—the set does not purport to *be* a real place, rather a representation, in the manner of a painting.

By 1879, Ibsen's view of stage design has changed dramatically, as evidenced by the level of detail—and, more importantly, the three-dimensionality—of the stage direction that begins *A Doll House:*

> A comfortable, tasteful but not expensively furnished room. A door to the right in the back wall leads out to the hall; another door to the left leads in to Helmer's study. Between these doors is a piano. In the middle of the left wall, a door, and farther back, a window. Near the window a round table with armchairs and a small sofa. In the right wall, upstage, a door and, on this same side nearer the foreground, a porcelain stove with a pair of armchairs and a rocking chair. Between the stove and the door, a little table. Engravings on the walls. An etagere with porcelain figures and other small art objects; a small bookcase with books in rich bindings. Carpet on the floor; the fire burns in the stove. A winter's day. (*A Doll House,* 1)

It is impossible to conceive of the room described here being accurately rendered in two-dimensional painted backdrops. Ibsen is imagining the entire world of the play in scenic terms, marking a profound shift in the aesthetics of stage design from a representational *background* against which the action of the play is carried out, to an *environment* in which the action takes place and which surrounds and supports that action rather than serving as illustration.

In this new way of imagining scenery, details in the decor begin to contribute to the overall system of symbols in the play. There are four visible doors in the set for *A Doll House* (along with an all-important fifth, the unseen exterior door through which Nora makes her famous final exit). Doors can be seen as a major symbolic element in the world of the play, keeping the outside world safely shut out from the Helmers' cozy home until it forces its way in—through the doors—in the persons of Mrs. Linde and Krogstad. And of course it is a door slam that signals the momentous, irrevocable departure of Nora from the Helmer household.

The piano, the *etagere* with small art objects, the engravings on the walls and the richly bound books all signal something important about the environment that Torvald and Nora have created: a middle-class world full of artistic gestures. These objects give the room a lived-in quality and reveal much about the tastes of the Helmers. Beyond the realistic revelation of character, however, there may be another function at work. As the action of the play unfolds, unmasking one illusion after another, Ibsen may be suggesting that the well-decorated, aesthetically pleasing room is, ironically, an insufficient fortress against the harsh realities of the world beyond those doors. The very furnishings of the room, then, serve as a means of symbolic communication.

How did Ibsen come to develop such a revolution in his thinking about the role of scenery in drama? As is often the case with large changes in artistic movements, the answer seems to lie in the collision of a number of forces operating simultaneously.

A shift toward greater realism in literature was already very much in the air by mid-century. Even in the comparative isolation of Bergen and Christiania, Ibsen was no doubt in touch with advances in European thinking through his work in the professional theatre.

A periodical with the title *Realisme* was founded in Paris in 1856 (Brockett and Findlay 7). Naturalism, which can be regarded as a logical extension of realism along scientific lines, gathered force after the publication of Darwin's *The Origin of Species* in 1859 and drew strength from the increasing clamor for the application of scientific methods to social problems (Brockett and Findlay 4). Ibsen left Norway in 1864 to live in Italy, beginning a long period of self-imposed exile from his native Norway. Living primarily in Rome, Ibsen got first-hand exposure to the literary and philosophical currents of the time (Meyer, vol. 2, ch. 1).

In 1873, Emile Zola scored a success with a dramatization of his own novel *Therese Raquin*, seen at the time as one of the first great examples of Naturalism in the theatre. His preface demonstrates the high seriousness of the movement toward greater realism and naturalism in the theatre

continued

continued

and offers a glimpse of some of the key artistic issues with which Zola was grappling:

> . . . We have now come to the birth of the true, that is the great, the only force of the century. Everything advances in a literary epoch. Whoever wishes to retreat or turn to one side will be lost in the general dust. This is why I am absolutely convinced that in the near future the Naturalist movement will take its place in the realm of the drama, and bring with it the power of reality, the new life of modern drama. . . .
>
> We must cast aside fables of every sort, and delve into the two-fold life of the character and its environment, bereft of every nursery tale, historical trapping, and the usual conventional stupidities. . . .
>
> I tried to make [*Therese Raquin*] a purely human study. . . . I tried continually to bring my setting into perfect accord with the occupations of my characters, in order that they might not *play*, but rather *live*, before the audience. (Zola, Preface to *Therese Raquin*, in Clark 377–8)

Zola's words may or may not have reached Ibsen in time to serve as a formative influence on the Norwegian playwright's shift from romance and history to socially engaged realism. Nevertheless, the preface to *Therese Raquin* signals an important intellectual current of which Ibsen, living by now in Dresden, could not have been unaware.

Another force was alive in the German theatre of the 1870s, creating a revolution in scenic detail and accuracy: the famous company of the Duke of Saxe-Meiningen. Ibsen's historical drama *The Pretenders* was staged by the Meininger troupe in 1876. The production seems to have gone well, at least from Ibsen's perspective, as he notes in a letter to his friend, the theatre manager and playwright Ludvig Josephson, dated 14 June, 1876:

> At the beginning of this month I went to Berlin, to be present at the first performance of *The Pretenders* [written by Ibsen in 1863], which was splendidly staged by the Court Theatrical Company of the Duke of Meiningen. The play was received with great applause, and I was called before the curtain several times. . . . After the first performance I was invited by the Duke to visit him at his castle of Liebenstein, near Meiningen, where I stayed until the day before yesterday. . . . (Morison 295)

This direct immersion in the work of a company and a director so renowned for the realism of their stagecraft might well have joined with the prevailing artistic winds of the time to speed the move Ibsen was already predisposed to make toward greater specificity in his scenic requirements. Ibsen biographer Michael Meyer thinks so:

Did the Meininger methods influence Ibsen's future writing? It is possible; the realism of that production of *The Pretenders* may well have had its effects on *The Pillars of Society*, which he was at last to complete during the following year [1877]. Mr. Peter Tennant suggests: "The setting and detail of the stage directions, with their references to gesture and expression, could almost have been taken out of a Meiningen producer's manuscript." (Meyer 2:220)

Clearly, all of the necessary forces are now gathered to move Ibsen decisively away from two-dimensional representations of generalized places and toward three-dimensional environments inhabited in very specific ways by his characters. His youthful experiences as a practical theatre producer, rebelling against the artificial staging conventions of the 1850s while absorbing the first stirrings of new thinking coming out of Germany and France, prepared the ground. His move to the European continent, first to Italy and then to Germany, immersed him in progressive thought about matters both artistic and political. Finally, his direct exposure to an innovative, even revolutionary theatre producer, the Duke of Saxe-Meiningen, showed him the power of detail and realism in scenic design. From there, it was a small step—though one with far-reaching consequences—to unite a three-dimensional conception of the stage to a rapidly maturing vision of the kind of play that that stage could hold.

Works Cited

Brockett, Oscar G., and Findlay, Robert R. *Century of Innovation: A History of European and American Theatre and Drama since 1870.* Englewood Cliffs, NJ: Prentice Hall, 1973.

Clark, Barrett H. *European Theories of the Drama.* New York: Crown, 1965.

Hemmer, Bjørn. "Ibsen the Dramatist." 1995. <http://home.sol.no/~abjerkho/grimstad/ibsentxt.htm>.

Ibsen, Henrik. *A Doll House*, translated by Rick Davis and Brian Johnston, in *Ibsen: Four Major Plays.* Lyme, NH: Smith and Kraus, 1995.

_____. *Love's Comedy*, translated by Jens Arup, in *The Oxford Ibsen*, vol. 2. London: Oxford UP, 1962.

Johnston, Brian. *To the Third Empire: Ibsen's Early Drama.* Minneapolis: University of Minnesota, 1980.

Meyer, Michael. *Henrik Ibsen, Vol. 1: The Making of a Dramatist.* London: Rupert Hart-Davis, 1967.

_____. *Henrik Ibsen. Vol. 2: The Farewell to Poetry.* London: Rupert Hart-Davis, 1971.

Morison, Mary, ed. *The Correspondence of Henrik Ibsen.* London: Hodder and Stoughton, 1905.

7

DRAMATIC THEORY AND THE THEATRICAL ESSAY

Sometimes the theatre compels us to ask larger questions than a review of a single play or the examination of a moment in theatre history can answer. Such questions become fodder for two other kinds of writing about theatre, **dramatic theory** and the **theatrical essay.** Often regarded as the exclusive domain of the professional scholar or critic, these forms can offer excellent opportunities for the student of theatre and drama to write serious, original studies of important aspects of the art form.

A work of theory and an essay are almost indistinguishable in certain instances, yet there are nuances of style that may help define a blurry line between them. If *theory* suggests an almost scientific rigor, the assertion and proof of certain principles about how drama works, the very word *essay* implies a kind of leisurely stroll through a garden of ideas, pausing at this interesting flower, turning unexpectedly down that branching path. The **theorist** typically focuses on a single issue, while the **essayist** may use the form to bring together observations, musings, and reflections that make very personal connections among multiple reference points.

The choice of **audience** also affects whether a given topic yields a work of dramatic theory or a theatrical essay. Theory is often written for an audience within the field, or with a certain level of *a priori* interest and expertise. The essay assumes a less specialized readership, with broad cultural interests but without any necessary experience in the field.

THEORY OR ESSAY? A CASE STUDY

As an example of how a single point of interest can develop into both a theory paper and a theatrical essay, imagine that you are growing increasingly aware of the influence of television on the current theatre. A dramatic theory approach to the subject might include a detailed breakdown of the structure of several TV programs and several contemporary plays. As a theorist, you could look at their act and scene breaks, the way the dramatic action is arranged—perhaps using the LOA diagram from Chapter 5 of this book—and the aesthetic implications of these structures. From such a comparison might emerge a theoretical framework for a discussion of the relationship between form and content: for example, how does the form of contemporary television and drama enforce certain kinds of content (or vice versa), and how does this compare to the same relationship in earlier (pretelevision) periods of dramatic writing?

Essayists might be teased by the same initial observation, but they are writing for an audience less specifically interested in theatre. The essay, therefore, might wonder whether societal factors are influencing—or being influenced by—the changing forms. The essay could recall the social adjustments created by television (e.g., the shift from public, communal viewings of plays and movies to private, "cocooned" experiences of TV programs), and speculate on the attention span required to watch an act of a play compared to a program that is interrupted every few minutes for commercials. The resulting essay, while touching many of the same points as the theoretical paper, will be written for a reader who may not be actively seeking an enhanced knowledge of dramatic structure but who is interested in the general subject of the relation between art and the culture at large.

PRACTICING THEORY: THE FRAMING QUESTIONS

If your task is to create a piece of original dramatic theory, a good way to begin is by contemplating the following set of **framing questions:**

- Why do we make theatre?
- What constitutes a "good" play or performance?
- What is the value of drama?
- How do plays and performances communicate meaning?
- How are plays and performances organized?
- What is the nature of representation?
- What is the relationship between text and performance?
- How does drama interact with society?

Almost every topic in dramatic theory, from the broadest consideration of theatrical structure to the most specific political reading of a given text, has its origin in one or more of these questions. We will return to one or more of these questions in each section of this chapter.

Two Roads, One Destination

There are two principal routes toward the development of a dramatic theory paper, and both use the framing questions as a guide: (1) *Collect a group of plays in which you are interested*—plays by one author, from one period, or (more challenging, perhaps) from across several periods or cultures—and begin asking questions of them, and (2) *Beginning with one or more of the framing questions, assemble a group of plays that helps provide evidence for the answer you're seeking.*

As you can see, these two processes are mirror images of each other, ultimately converging on the same sets of data. The difference is in the starting point: recognizing that good writing in dramatic theory requires a personal investment in the questions being asked.

Texts ⟶ Questions ⟶ Theory

You might, for example, have a strong response to plays by American women in the twentieth century. You have read, let's say, some works by Rachel Crothers, Susan Glaspell, Gertrude Stein, Alice Childress, Lillian Hellman, Lorraine Hansberry, Wendy Wasserstein, and Suzan-Lori Parks, and you are struck in a still-indefinable way by a sense of connectedness among these very different writers and their disparate texts.

Translating this response—whether it's enthusiasm, respect, curiosity, unease, or something else—into **theory** requires a process of questioning. Begin by interrogating your own response as fully as possible, in a **personal inventory** that might include something like the following questions:

- Why do I feel engaged by this group of plays and writers?
- What about them suggests connection (e.g., structure, subject, character, language?)
- What differentiates them?
- What prior theoretical constructions (or biases) do I bring to the table, and are they valid for this group of plays?

These questions might be excellent starting points for entries in a **reading response log,** as described in Chapter 2.

Then try applying one or more of the framing questions. You will probably find that certain of the questions create more resonant responses when applied to your chosen group of texts; follow that lead in your log and explore ways in which the framing questions help create connections among your chosen texts. In so doing, you will be creating the dummy draft of your dramatic theory paper (see Chapter 3 for an explanation of this stage of the writing process). The result will most likely be rather schematic and categorical, but it will serve well to organize your thinking so that your later writing will retain a sense of order appropriate to the dramatic theory task.

New Questions, New Answers

Obviously, the focus of the resulting study will change depending on which of the framing questions you choose to ask. Considering the group of plays suggested, a paper focusing on the questions "How are plays and performances organized?" and "How do plays and performances communicate meaning?" might lead to some controversial theoretical inquiries into gender-specific structural tendencies. A paper addressing "What is the value of drama?" or "How does drama interact with society?" might use this group of writers and their plays to talk about changing gender roles in society as a whole, including their depictions on the stage.

Questions —→ Texts —→ Theory: An Alternate Route

You might, on the other hand, be initially engaged not by the texts themselves but by one of the framing questions, such as "Why do we make theatre?" (along with its inevitable corollary, "How does drama interact with society?"). Recognizing that no single study can address these questions for all times and places, you will begin thinking about a group of writers and plays that could provide a containable case study. In this procedure, the *question* is the starting point, the energizing force for the inquiry; the body of evidence is chosen to provide a focused exploration of the subject.

The same group listed (or a more limited subset of it—let's say, those American women writers working in the first half of the twentieth century) might come to mind as illustrative of a time when "making theatre," for these writers, was an act of unusual courage, a departure from the expected societal norms. American women playwrights in the first half of the twentieth century could not expect to make a living at their craft and could not even reasonably expect social and cultural approval for their work. Why, then, this impulse to create in a form that would seem to be hostile to their efforts? How did it affect their work? What does this say about the impulse toward theatremaking?

These examples demonstrate two ways to organize a theory paper in response to the same set of data. The first takes the texts as a point of departure and applies the framing questions to them; the second begins with the framing questions and proceeds to apply the texts. The resulting studies, argued from the same body of work, would no doubt take significantly different shapes, but both would be valid expressions of dramatic theory.

The key is to determine your own most intense point of engagement with the subject (put another way, what bothers you or excites you most? What do you find yourself *needing* to think about?) and construct your paper accordingly.

Standards of Evidence in Dramatic Theory

In crafting dramatic theory, the important thing is to be clear about both the questions being asked and the textual support for each step in an advancing argument. Theory requires a high standard of evidence; every assertion should be defensible according to the practices of good argumentation. If it is impossible to "prove" anything in the always-subjective world of literature and performance, the dramatic theorist comes closest to achieving that impossibility by thorough testing and careful articulation of each step of the reasoning process. Following the stages of the writing process described in Chapter 3, particularly obtaining detailed "feedback" on your work-in-progress from knowledgeable readers, is an essential way to test your reasoning against high standards.

Theory Rolls Up Its Sleeves

Another kind of dramatic theory paper offers to analyze (and/or diagnose) how plays succeed or fail as texts or in actual performance. The framing question that applies most directly to this area is "What constitutes a 'good' play or performance?" The theorist tries to find out the underlying principles that make drama communicate in an effort to understand why certain plays and productions exert a powerful effect (they "work") and others do not.

Prescriptive versus Descriptive Theory

In pursuit of this kind of theory, writers may adopt two distinctly different strategies, often called descriptive and prescriptive theory. **Descriptive theory** seeks to understand the elements of drama as they exist in a given work or set of works. The theorist may then propose that certain elements are more or less successful in creating a dramatic effect.

Aristotle's *Poetics* is largely a work of descriptive theory, analyzing the component parts of tragedy, placing them in a hierarchy of importance, but avoiding (for the most part) positive assertions of how to write a play. His stance is roughly this: Here's a successful play (in his case, the *Oedipus Rex* of Sophocles); here's how it works; plays written with these elements in mind will also work.

Prescriptive theory, by contrast, seeks a more definitive statement: Here's how it *should* be done. A prescriptive theorist (often an artist as well) suggests new ways in which plays might be organized, going well beyond a description of already-existing forms. Prescriptive theory is typically somewhat more polemical, seeking to bring about a change in the way plays are constructed, performed, or viewed.

In the sixteenth and seventeenth centuries, for example, neoclassical theorists refined and extended Aristotle's observations into strict prescriptions for playwriting. In the contemporary era, many of Bertolt Brecht's writings are prescriptive, especially works like *A Short Organum for the Theater*, in which the master playwright details a set of principles for text and performance; other twentieth-century examples include Antonin Artaud's "No More Masterpieces" and F. T. Marinetti's "Futurist Manifesto," which call for fundamental changes in the way art is made.

Writing Practical Theory

To write a work of what we might call "practical theory," first take a hard look at your purpose:

- Is it descriptive or prescriptive, or some combination of the two?
- If your approach is descriptive, what source texts will you choose to analyze? What are their exemplary features? Why are these features significant (worthy of study, emulation, or challenge?)
- If your approach is prescriptive, what is the goal of your prescription? What changes do you want to effect in the way drama is made? Why are these new principles necessary?

Again, we suggest you use a log to explore these topics, then follow the steps of the writing process described in Chapter 3 toward turning your explorations into a well-organized, well-argued paper.

Theory and Society

Since drama and theatre have always existed in a social context, theorists have been interested in the sociopolitical impact of the art form since, at least, the time of Plato. A great deal of energy has been given to attacking and defending the theatre through the ages, typically on battlefields defined by morality and civic virtue. Jonas Barish's excellent study, *The Antitheatrical Prejudice*, examines attacks on the theatre's role within society (and, sometimes, its very right to exist) by philosophers, religious figures, and politicians.

Are these writings—and the responses they elicit, often from the pens of the artists under attack—dramatic theory? It would seem so, since they engage many of the **framing questions** set out on p. 89, especially "What is the value of drama?" and "How does drama interact with society?"

Both the attackers and defenders often marshal textual evidence to support their points of view, and sometimes that evidence is surprisingly acute. For example, it was a long time before scholars successfully countered Rev. Jeremy Collier's attack on Restoration comedy in "A Short View of the Immorality and Profaneness of the English Stage," a 1698 pamphlet that used the principle of poetic justice to suggest that the comedies encouraged public immorality by rewarding vice and punishing virtue in their plots.

Historical debates about the role of theatre in society can provide a rich background for the writer of contemporary dramatic theory. The ways in which drama and theatre are written, performed, funded, and attended in today's world are being argued over in pulpits and legislatures, and it can be instructive to try to discover the seeds of modern controversies in old battles.

Objections raised to the propriety of certain "performance artists" working at the end of the twentieth century—for example, Karen Finley, Holly Hughes, the PoMo Afro Homos—might be compared to the unease created by actors in the days of the early Christian church, or the cloud of suspicion that hung over the introduction of women to the English stage in 1660. Jean-Jacques Rousseau's arguments against the founding of a theatre in Geneva in 1758 offer a striking precursor to the ongoing debate about the proper role of government in the arts in today's society. The dramatic theorist might frame a question around what makes the act of performance inherently threatening to certain moral and political values and then attempt to discover whether our current difficulties in accepting various performers and styles have roots in the past.

Dramatic theory also has intersections with the major sociopolitical issues of our time. While it is outside the scope of this book to survey the range of those issues, it is worth noting that such fields as gender studies, ethnic studies, economics, anthropology, political science, and studies that integrate art forms (breaking down disciplinary lines between, for example, dance and theatre) have all contributed significantly to the constellation of approaches to contemporary dramatic theory.

THE THEATRICAL ESSAY

Writing the theatrical essay should be an act of pure pleasure. The form is without a set of rules or guidelines; the shape of an individual essay will be determined by the writer's choice of **subject, audience,** and **purpose.** As an exercise in the graceful expression of a firmly held conviction, the essay can serve as a useful assignment in any number of courses from dramatic literature to composition.

Developing a Subject

The subject can develop out of the same kind of inventory of personal interests suggested in this chapter. What is it about theatre and drama that excites/angers/engages/bothers/bores/moves you?

Some writers find it helpful to keep a **journal** or **log,** either in a traditional notebook form or some other collection of retrievable notes (such as a computer file, a bulletin board, a box of index cards), to preserve observations, insights, references, and essay ideas for later development. This journal is a variant of the reading response log described in Chapter 2. No observation should be considered too small to include in the journal. The creative combination of seemingly disparate ideas is one very powerful engine of original thinking, and collecting ideas in a journal or log is an excellent way of enabling that process to work.

The **framing questions** listed on page 89 can be just as useful in developing a point of view for a theatrical essay as they are for dramatic theory. One good procedure is to consult the list of questions periodically as you review or add to the contents of your journal; holding both a question and a set of observations in mind simultaneously can lead to new connections and possible subjects for an essay.

The Audience

While practicing the theatrical essay can be useful in many school contexts, this form is best known from its appearances in diverse publications. The nature of the audience for a theatrical essay depends on the kind of publication in which the essay appears. As with dramatic criticism/play reviews, there are several primary venues for the essay: newspapers (typically in a magazine or a Sunday arts section), weekly and monthly magazines, and quarterly journals. Theatrical essays also appear frequently in book-length collections, often of previously published pieces.

If you are creating an imaginary audience or have a choice of assigned audiences, consider the limitations and possibilities of each of the above publications. A Sunday newspaper may reach millions of readers (and, if it's a major paper such as the *New York Times,* it will have national distribution), but it may place certain limits on the complexity of ideas presented and will certainly have finite space restrictions. Monthly magazines and journals are less likely to limit either space or content, and while they will likely reach a smaller audience, that audience will probably bring a higher level of engagement with your subject to their reading. In either case, it is vital to know who your audience is and to write with an appropriate level of detail and complexity (see Audience in Chapter 3).

Purpose

The essay form invites a highly personal style of writing and has a wide range of possible subjects, so it is all the more essential to develop a clear sense of purpose for the piece. Just as an actor often states an objective in the form of an infinitive verb, a writer can develop a concise infinitive statement for an essay. The goal might be **to persuade** the reader of the worth of

Playwright X, **to make a connection** between social trend Y and new play Z, or **to criticize** the quality of production at theatres 1, 2, and 3. Stating a purpose helps activate the subject and gives the writer a guide to the most suitable tone and style of the essay (see Purpose in Chapter 3).

Some Possible Subjects

While there is no limit to the number of possible subjects for the theatrical essay—and, in fact, all of the issues raised in connection with dramatic theory in the preceding pages would also make for fine essays—the following list offers some ideas as springboards for development of original writing:

- *The role of the director:* When does "interpretation" become "rewriting"? (Or: director versus *auteur.*)
- *Great acting:* What is it, and how do you recognize it?
- *Contemporary theatre and . . . :* Select a social or political issue—such as race, gender, class, religion—and discuss how theatre and drama respond to it.
- *Supporting theatre (and the other arts):* Public versus private funding.
- *Film and theatre:* How do they influence each other? Consider visual style, language, economics, the audience, other issues.
- *Alternative styles of theatre:* These include the development of performance art, private performances, media and theatre.

Sample Excerpts: Brecht and Bentley

The following brief excerpts may help to illustrate the similarities and differences between a work of dramatic theory and a theatrical essay. The first, from Bertolt Brecht's lecture *On Experimental Theatre*, sets out a rationale for a new purpose for theatre and drama, calling upon classical precedents for support. This is a work of both **descriptive** and **prescriptive** theory, and Brecht applies at least two of the **framing questions**—"Why do we make theatre?" and "What constitutes a 'good' play or production?"—in developing his argument.

> . . . Bourgeois revolutionary aesthetics, founded by such great figures of the Enlightenment as Diderot and Lessing, defines the theatre as a place of entertainment and instruction. During the Enlightenment, a period which saw the start of a tremendous upsurge of the European theatre, there was no conflict between these two things. Pure amusement, provoked even by objects of tragedy, struck men like Diderot as utterly hollow and unworthy unless it added something to the

spectators' knowledge, while elements of instruction, in artistic form of course, seemed in no wise to detract from the amusement; in these men's view they gave depth to it.

If we now look at the theatre of our day we shall find an increasingly marked conflict between the two elements which go to make it up, together with its plays—entertainment and instruction. Today there is an opposition here. That "assimilation of art to science" which gave naturalism its social influence undoubtedly hamstrung some major artistic capacities, notably the imagination, the sense of play and the element of pure poetry. Its artistic aspects were clearly harmed by its instructive side.

The expressionism of the postwar period showed the World as Will and Idea and led to a special kind of solipsism. It was the theatre's answer to the great crisis of society just as the doctrines of Mach were philosophy's. It represented art's revolt against life: here the world existed purely as a vision, strangely distorted, a monster conjured up by perturbed souls. Expressionism vastly enriched the theatre's means of expression and brought aesthetic gains that still have to be fully exploited, but it proved quite incapable of shedding light on the world as an object of human activity. The theatre's educative value collapsed. . . .*

The next excerpt offers an example of a writer dealing with some of the same questions in the form of a theatrical essay. Here Eric Bentley, himself a noted translator and critic of Brecht, takes up the question of the function of drama. Notice how the tone and style of the essay differ from the more theoretical approach that Brecht employs; Bentley allows his writing to be more personal and anecdotal, and he seems to be speaking more directly to the reader.

. . . People speak of political theatre as very special. But in the theatre anything can become political by a sudden turn of events outside the theatre. During World War I, there was a potato shortage in England, so that when the line "Let the sky rain potatoes!" came up in a Shakespeare production, the audience rose to its feet and applauded. Now that was political theatre—momentarily. And it would be political theatre if an anti-Semitic regime decided to celebrate its accession to power with a gala performance of *The Merchant of Venice*.

---

*Excerpt from "On Experimental Theatre" from *Brecht on Theatre* edited and translated by John Willett. Translation copyright © 1964 and copyright renewed © 1992 by John Willett. Reprinted by permission of Hill and Wang, a division of Farrar, Straus & Giroux, Inc.

I would not want to define politics so broadly that all art is political. That is as unfruitful a proposition as that no art is political. Much drama that people loosely call political might better be termed social, just as what is often meant by sexual politics is no different from sexual sociology. It would be more sensible, I think, to limit the term political to works in which the question of the power structure arises. . . .

. . . Most writing, most literature, most art, is only the opium of the people, is but the intellectual equivalent of our politics and economics. The *New York Post* (founded in 1801 by Alexander Hamilton) is literature, and at that the most widely read. Minds which deal in moral risk, formal experimentation, et cetera, are not represented in it, or in the most widely read fiction, or even, probably, in the most widely read poetry. As for the most widely consumed drama, that is situation comedy on television. And here I'd like to mention again the theoretical opposition which the entertainment industry offers to propaganda. In practice, *all* their entertainment is propaganda, either by directly validating the status quo, or by offering convenient evasions of it. . . . *

---

*From "Writing for a Political Theatre," by Eric Bentley, 1985. Copyright © 1985 by Eric Bentley. *Thinking about the Playwright*. (Evanston, IL: Northwestern UP, 1987) pp. 186–187.

8

SOURCES FOR RESEARCH IN THEATRE AND HOW TO CITE THEM

This chapter is in two parts. The first presents a selected list of sources, both print (books, periodicals, reference works, etc.) and electronic (Internet and Websites) in each of the areas of theatre and drama scholarship we have covered in this book. The second part of the chapter is a guide to proper citation of sources in your papers and articles. We use the standards of the Modern Language Association, whose manual of style is preferred in the arts and humanities. The research paper in theatre history presented in Chapter 6 is documented according to Modern Language Association (MLA) style.

THEATRE BIBLIOGRAPHY

Compiled by Rick Davis and Brian Barker.

Theatre History—Books

Barish, Jonas A. *The Antitheatrical Prejudice.* Berkeley: University of California Press, 1981.

Berthold, Margot. *The History of World Theater: From the Beginnings to the Baroque.* Trans. Edith Simmons. New York: Continuum, 1991.

Bordman, Gerald Martin. *American Musical Theatre: A Chronicle.* New York: Oxford University Press, 1978.

Brockett, Oscar G. *The Essential Theatre.* Fort Worth, TX: Harcourt Brace College Publishers, 1996.

_____. *History of Theatre.* Boston: Allyn and Bacon, 1995.

_____, and Robert R. Findlay. *Century of Innovation: A History of European and American Theatre and Drama since 1870.* Englewood Cliffs, NJ: Prentice Hall, 1973.

Brown, John Russell, ed. *Oxford Illustrated History of Theatre.* New York: Oxford UP, 1995.

Grose, Donald B., and O. Franklin Kenworthy. *A Mirror to Life: A History of Western Theater.* New York: Holt, Rinehart and Winston, 1985.

Hartnoll, Phyllis. *The Theatre: A Concise History.* New York: Thames and Hudson, 1985.

Henderson, Mary. *Theater in America: 200 Years of Plays, Players, and Productions.* New York: Abrams, 1986.

Hill, Errol, ed. *The Theater of Black Americans.* New York: Applause, 1987.

Kernodle, George Riley. *The Theatre in History.* Fayetteville, AR: University of Arkansas Press, 1989.

Mitchley, Jack, and Peter Spalding. *Five Thousand Years of Theatre.* New York: Holmes & Meier, 1982.

Nagler, A. M. *Sources of Theatrical History.* New York: Dover, 1952.

Rubin, Don, ed. *The World Encyclopedia of Contemporary Theatre.* New York: Routledge, 1994.

Shipley, Joseph Twadell. *The Crown Guide to the World's Great Plays, from Ancient Greece to Modern Times.* New York: Crown, 1984.

Watson, Jack, and Grant McKernie. *A Cultural History of Theatre.* New York: Longman, 1993.

Theatre History—Periodicals

The Drama Review. New York: New York University School of Arts, 1955/57–.

Nineteenth Century Theatre Research. Tucson, AZ: J. P. Wearing, 1973–1986.

Restoration and 18th Century Theatre Research. Chicago: Loyola University of Chicago, 1963–.

Studies in American Drama, 1945–Present. Erie, PA: Philip C. Kolin and Colby H. Kullman, 1986–1993.

Theatre History Studies. Grand Forks: University of North Dakota Press, 1981–.

Theatre Journal. Baltimore, MD: Johns Hopkins UP, 1979–.

Theatre Notebook. London: Society for Theatre Research, 1945–.

Play Analysis—Books

Ball, David. *Backwards and Forwards: A Technical Manual for Reading Plays.* Carbondale, IL: Southern Illinois UP, 1983.

Esslin, Martin. *An Anatomy of Drama.* New York: Hill and Wang, 1976.

Gross, Roger. *Understanding Playscripts: Theory and Method.* Bowling Green, OH: Bowling Green State UP, 1974.

Grote, David. *Script Analysis: Reading and Understanding the Playscript for Production.* Belmont, CA: Wadsworth, 1985.

Hayman, Ronald. *How to Read a Play.* New York: Grove Press, 1977.

Martin, Jacqueline. *Understanding Theatre: Performance Analysis in Theory and Practice.* Stockholm: Almqvist & Wiksell, 1995.

Pickering, Thomas, Kenneth Pickering, and David Bradby. *Studying Drama: A Handbook.* London: Croom Helm, 1983.

Ratliff, Gerald Lee. *Playscript Interpretation and Production.* New York: Rosen, 1985.

Schlueter, June. *Dramatic Closure: Reading the End.* Madison, NJ: Farleigh Dickinson UP, 1995.

Play Analysis—Periodicals

American Theatre. New York: Theatre Communications Group, 1984–.
Comparative Drama. Kalamazoo, MI: Comparative Drama, 1967–.
The Drama Review. New York: New York University School of Arts, 1955/57–.
Journal of Dramatic Theory and Criticism. Lawrence, KS: University of Kansas, 1986–.
Modern Drama. Toronto: A. M. Hakkert Ltd., 1958–.
Theater. New Haven, CT: Yale School of Drama, 1977–.
Theatre Topics. Baltimore, MD: Johns Hopkins UP, 1991–.
Yale/Theatre. New Haven, CT: Yale School of Drama, 1968–1977.

Drama Criticism and Theory—Books

Adams, Henry Hitch, and Baxter Hataway, ed. *Dramatic Essays of the Neoclassic Age.* New York: Columbia UP, 1950.

Artaud, Antonin. *The Theater and Its Double.* Trans. Mary Caroline. New York: Grove Press, 1958.

Beckerman, Bernard. *Dynamics of Drama: Theory and Method of Analysis.* New York: Drama Book Specialists, 1979.

Bennet, Benjamin. *Theater as Problem: Modern Drama and Its Place in Literature.* Ithaca, NY: Cornell UP, 1990.

Bentley, Eric. *The Life of the Drama.* New York: Athenaeum, 1964.

_____. *The Theatre of Commitment: and Other Essays on Drama in Our Society.* New York: Atheneum, 1967.

_____. *The Theory of the Modern Stage: An Introduction to Modern Theatre and Drama.* New York: Penguin, 1968.

Blau, Herbert. *The Audience.* Baltimore, MD: Johns Hopkins UP, 1990.

_____. *To All Appearances: Ideology and Performance.* New York: Routledge, 1992.

Brecht, Bertolt. *Brecht on Theatre; The Development of an Aesthetic.* Ed. and Trans. John Willett. New York: Hill and Wang, 1996.

Brustein, Robert. *Critical Moments: Reflections on Theater and Society, 1973–1979.* New York: Random House, 1980.

_____. *The Culture Watch: Essays on Theatre and Society, 1969–1974.* New York: Knopf, 1975.

_____. *Reimagining American Theatre.* New York: Hill and Wang, 1991.

_____. *The Theatre of Revolt: An Approach to the Modern Drama.* Boston: Little, Brown, 1964.

_____. *Who Needs Theatre: Dramatic Opinions.* New York: Atlantic Monthly, 1987.

Campbell, Paul Newell. *Form and the Art of the Theatre.* Bowling Green, OH: Bowling Green State UP, 1984.

Carlson, Marvin A. *Theories of the Theatre: A Historical and Critical Survey from the Greeks to the Present.* Ithaca, NY: Cornell UP, 1993.

Case, Sue-Ellen et al., ed. *Cruising the Performative: Interventions into the Representation of Ethnicity, Nationality, and Sexuality.* Bloomington: Indiana UP, 1995.

Case, Sue-Ellen. *Feminism and Theatre.* New York: Methuen, 1988.

_____, ed. *Performing Feminisms: Feminist Critical Theory and Theatre.* Baltimore: Johns Hopkins UP, 1990.

Chaudhuri, Una. *Staging Place: The Geography of Modern Drama.* Ann Arbor: University of Michigan Press, 1995.

Davidson, Clifford, C. J. Gianakaris, and John Stroupe, eds. *Drama in the Twentieth Century: Comparative and Critical Essays.* New York: AMS Press, 1984.

Diamond, Elin. *Performance and Cultural Politics.* London: Routledge, 1996.

Dukore, Bernard Frank, comp. *Dramatic Theory and Criticism: Greeks to Grotowski.* New York: Holt, Rinehart and Winston, 1974.

Gilman, Richard. *The Confusion of Realms.* New York: Random House, 1969.

_____. *The Making of Modern Drama: A Study of Büchner, Ibsen, Strindberg, Chekhov, Pirandello, Brecht, Beckett, Handke.* New York: Farrar, Straus and Giroux, 1974.

Fuchs, Elinor. *The Death of Character: Perspectives on Theater after Modernism.* Bloomington: Indiana UP, 1996.

Kauffmann, Stanley. *Persons of the Drama: Theater Criticism and Comment.* New York: Harper & Row, 1976.

_____. *Theater Criticisms.* New York: Performing Arts Journal, 1983.

Kerr, Walter. *Journey to the Center of the Theater.* New York: Knopf, 1979.

_____. *Pieces at Eight.* New York: Dutton, 1968.

_____. *The Theater in Spite of Itself.* New York: Simon and Schuster, 1963.

_____. *Thirty Plays Hath November: Pain and Pleasure in the Contemporary Theater.* New York: Simon and Schuster, 1969.

Kott, Jan. *The Theater of Essence and Other Essays.* Evanston, IL: Northwestern UP, 1984.

Malekin, Peter. *Consciousness, Literature, and Theatre: Theory and Beyond.* New York: St. Martin's Press, 1997.

Marowitz, Charles. *Alarums & Excursions: Our Theatres in the Nineties.* New York: Applause, 1996.

Marranca, Bonnie. *Ecologies of Theater: Essays at the Century Turning.* Baltimore: Johns Hopkins UP, 1996.

_____, ed. *The Theatre of Images.* Baltimore: Johns Hopkins UP, 1996.

Martin, Jacqueline. *Understanding Theater: Performance Analysis in Theory and Practice.* Stockholm: Almqvist & Wiskell, 1995.

Meister, Charles W. *Dramatic Criticism: A History.* Jefferson, NC: McFarland, 1985.

Miller, Arthur. *The Theater Essays of Arthur Miller.* Ed. Robert A. Martin. New York: Penguin, 1978.

Nicoll, Alladyce. *The Theatre and Dramatic Theory.* New York: Barnes & Noble, 1962.

Palmer, Richard H. *The Critic's Canon: Standards of Theatrical Reviewing in America.* New York: Greenwood, 1988.

Rogoff, Gordon. *Theatre Is Not Safe.* Evanston, IL: Northwestern UP, 1987.

Rogowski, Christian. *Implied Dramaturgy: Robert Musil and the Crisis of Modern Drama.* Riverside, CA: Ariadne, 1993.

Schechner, Richard. *Public Domain: Essays on the Theater*. Indianapolis: Bobbs-Merrill, 1969.

Sontag, Susan. *Against Interpretation and Other Essays*. New York: Anchor, 1966.

States, Bert O. *The Pleasure of Play*. Ithaca, NY: Cornell UP, 1994.

Trudeau, Lawrence J. *Drama Criticism: Criticism of the Most Significant and Widely Studied Dramatic Works from All the World's Literatures*. Detroit: Gale Research, 1991.

Vena, Gary. *How to Read and Write about Drama*. New York: Arco, 1988.

Wadle, Irving. *Theatre Criticism*. New York: Routledge, 1992.

Wolter, Jurgen, ed. *The Dawning of American Drama: American Dramatic Criticism*. Westport, CT: Greenwood, 1993.

Drama Criticism, Theory, and Essays—Periodicals

American Theatre. New York: Theatre Communications Group, 1984–.

Comparative Drama. Kalamazoo, MI: Comparative Drama, 1967–.

Drama Review. New York: New York University School of Arts, 1955/57–.

Journal of Dramatic Theory and Criticism. Lawrence, KS: University of Kansas, 1986–.

Modern Drama. Toronto: A. M. Hakkert, 1958–.

Nineteenth Century Theatre Research. Tucson, AZ: J. P. Wearing, 1973–1986.

Performing Arts Journal. New York: Performing Arts Journal, 1976–.

Studies in American Drama, 1945–Present. Erie, PA: Philip C. Kolin and Colby H. Kullman, 1986–1993.

Theater. New Haven, CT: Yale School of Drama, 1977–.

Theatre Journal. Washington: American Theatre Association, 1979.

Theatre Research International. London: Oxford UP, 1975–.

Theatre Topics. Baltimore, MD: Johns Hopkins UP, 1991–.

Yale/Theatre. New Haven, CT: Yale School of Drama, 1968–1977.

Dictionaries

Bowman, Walter Parker. *Theatre Language: A Dictionary of Terms in English of the Drama and Stage from Medieval to Modern Times*. New York: Theatre Arts, 1961.

Hodgson, Terry. *The Drama Dictionary*. New York: New Amsterdam, 1988.

Trapido, Joel, ed. *An International Dictionary of Theatre Language*. Westport, CT: Greenwood, 1985.

Encyclopedias

Banham, Martin, ed. *The Cambridge Guide to World Theatre*. Cambridge: Cambridge UP, 1988.

Bordman, Gerald Martin. *The Oxford Companion to American Theatre*. 2nd ed. New York: Oxford UP, 1992.

Esslin, Martin, ed. *The Encyclopedia of World Theater*. Intro. Esslin. New York: Scribner, 1977.

Hartnoll, Phyllis, ed. *The Oxford Companion to the Theatre*. 4th ed. Oxford: Oxford UP, 1983.

Hochman, Stanley, ed. *McGraw-Hill Encyclopedia of World Drama: An International Reference Work*. New York: McGraw-Hill, 1984.

Wilmeth, Don B., and Tice L. Miller, eds. *Cambridge Guide to American Theatre*. Cambridge: Cambridge UP, 1993.

Literature Guides and Bibliographies

Bailey, Claudia Jean. *A Guide to Reference and Bibliography for Theatre Research*. 2nd ed. Columbus: Ohio State U Library, Publ. Comm., 1983.

Salem, James M. *A Guide to Critical Reviews*. 3rd ed. Metuchen, NJ: Scarecrow, 1984–1991.

Silvester, Robert. *United States Theatre: A Bibliography: From the Beginning to 1990*. New York: Motley, 1993.

Stevens, David G. *English Renaissance Theatre History: A Reference Guide*. Boston: G. K. Hall, 1982.

Taylor, Thomas J. *American Theatre History: An Annotated Bibliography*. Pasadena, CA: Salem, 1992.

World Wide Web Addresses

Jam! Theatre. <http://www.canoe.ca/Theatre/>
Playbill On-Line. <http://www1.playbill.com/playbill/>
Theatre Communications Group. <http://www.tcg.org>
Theatre Links. <http://ivtours.com/theatre/links.htm>
Theatrenet. <http://www.theatrenet.co.uk/>
Theatre Perspectives International. <http: //www.tesser.com/tpi/>
Theatre Topics. <http://muse.jhu.edu/journals/tt/index.html>
World Wide Art Resources. <http://wwar.com/theater/perform.html>

RULES FOR CITATION OF SOURCES

The following section shows how to cite many different kinds of sources correctly using Modern Language Association (MLA) style. First, we show how to cite sources correctly within the text of your paper or article. Second, we show how to cite sources correctly in the "Works Cited" page(s) which follow your text. See the documented research paper in Chapter 6 for an example of proper construction of a "Works Cited" page(s), as well as correct citation within the text.

Note that your "Works Cited" page(s) should include *all* sources that you have cited in your paper or article and *only* those sources you have cited. The "Works Cited" section does *not* include other sources you may have consulted in your research; nor does it include other sources that you might suggest for your reader to consult. If your professor or editor requests it, you can add a page of "Other Works Consulted" or "Suggested

Further Reading"; however, such lists should never be confused with your "Works Cited" page(s).

The "Works Cited" section should be constructed **alphabetically by the author's last name** (see the examples in the guide for exceptions; e.g., when the author is unknown or there are multiple authors). The first line of any citation should begin at the **left margin;** subsequent lines of a citation should be **indented.**

For more information about MLA documentation (though not specific to Theatre and Drama), consult *The MLA Handbook for Writers of Research Papers,* 4th edition (New York: Modern Language Association, 1995). On the World Wide Web, literally dozens of Websites can be found which list examples of MLA citation style (use the search term "Modern Language Association"). These are not official sites of the Association; many are sponsored by college and university libraries and writing centers.

MLA In-Text Citation Guide

Examples compiled by Brian Barker.

An Author in the Text

If you wish to emphasize the author of a work, name the author in your sentence. A parenthetical citation is not required, unless your reference is to a specific page(s) in that source.

> Critic Steve Quinton recognizes Eugene O'Neill's use of dramatic structure in creating a play's meaning.

An Author in a Parenthetical Reference

Use a parenthetical reference when you wish to focus on a source's information, but not its author. In this example, the play is referred to as a whole, so no page numbers are needed in the reference. Note that the period comes after the parenthetical reference.

> The play *Desire Under the Elms* is only one example of modern drama's addressing the Oedipus myth (O'Neill).

When a particular part of the source is referenced, provide the author's name and page number(s) in your parenthetical reference. If you name the author in your sentence, you only need to provide the page numbers in the reference.

> When King Lear lashes out at and releases his anger on his daughters, he displaces himself and refuses to acknowledge his role in the conflict (Benjamin 56).

Paul Benjamin suggests that King Lear displaces his anger on his daughters and refuses to take responsibility for the situation at hand (56).

In using a quotation from a source, the parenthetical reference falls outside of the quotation marks, but before the end punctuation.

Robert Wise suggests that Iago contributes to Othello's fall by using "his wit to distort reality and lies to conjure up illusions" (3).

The exception to the preceding rule occurs when the quotation closes with an exclamation point or question mark. Leave these types of punctuation within the quotes, but still place a period after the parenthetical reference.

In exploring the popularity and continuing production of Shakespeare's plays in the twentieth century, Joseph Papp and Elizabeth Kirkland ask, "Is it the themes he addresses? Is it that the human dilemmas he explores transcend specific centuries and particular civilizations?" (189–190).

A Block Quotation

In a block quotation, the parenthetical reference follows the closing punctuation mark.

In examining the role of Shakespeare in our society, Levin suggests that:

> Shakespeare's works have been
> accorded a place in our culture above and
> beyond their topmost place in our literature.
> They have been virtually canonized as
> humanistic scriptures, the tested residue of
> pragmatic wisdom, a general collection of
> quotable texts and usable examples. (1)

A Source with Two or Three Authors

In this case, no matter if the reference is in the text or parenthetical, provide all the names of the authors.

A daunting obstacle in sixteenth century play production was the Master of Revels. He possessed the authority to censor any material that criticized government policies or the Church of England (Papp and Kirkland 147).

A Source by Four or More Authors
In this case, you may provide the lead author's name and the abbreviation et al. ("and others").

> When considering the quality of a performance, one must consider all aspects of the play, not just the acting (Bowden et al. 318).

Two or More Works with the Same Author
For clarity, use a parenthetical reference with an abbreviated form of the cited title.

> Middleton addresses the aspect of sexual currency in such plays as *The Changeling* and *Women Beware Women*. Thus, it is no surprise when Leantio describes his new wife Bianca's sexuality as ample dowry (*Women* 1.1.54–56).

Authors with the Same Last Name
When authors have the same last name, use a first initial(s) to distinguish them.

> A review in the *Lexington Herald* described Hopkins' performance as "inspired" and "legendary" (B. Rogers C2). However, the review in the *Times* criticized him for "forced emotion . . . bordering on melodrama" (S. T. Rogers D3).

Two or More Works in One Citation
In this case, use semicolons to divide the works.

> Many critics agree that Laurence Olivier's portrayal of Hamlet stands as the most compelling to date (Stevens; Cox; Smith).

A Multivolume Work
In referencing a page in a multivolume work, provide the volume number using an arabic numeral. The volume number and page number are separated by a colon and a space.

> Edward Albee, an American playwright, was born in 1928 (Willis 2: 12).

A Literary Work
Some older, more famous literary works may have several editions. For these types of references, provide information for the work itself and not for specific editions, except when you are focusing on a particular contribution of the edition. In citing parts of a play, give the act, scene, and line numbers in arabic numerals.

Othello's love for Desdemona seems to have completely dissipated
when he rages:

> All fond love thus do I blow to heaven
> 'Tis gone.
> Arise black vengeance from the hollow hell!
> Yield up, O love, thy crown and hearted throne,
> To tyrannous hate. (*Othello* 3.4.445–449)

In referencing an editor's contribution, shift the focus of your reference. In
the example here, *n* represents *note.*

In the *Riverside Shakespeare*, the editor's note stating that an "union" is a
fine pearl, clarifies the passage in which Claudius plots, "The King
shall drink to Hamlet's better breath,/ And in the cup an union shall he
throw" (*Hamlet* 4.2.271–272n).

Information in a Secondhand Source

In quoting original material from a secondhand source, cite the source using the abbreviation *qtd. in* (quoted in).

Bernard Shaw noted: "The modern Irish theatre began with *Cathleen Ni
Houlihan* of Mr. Yeats and Lady Gregory's *Rising of the Moon*, in which
the old patriotism stirred and wrung its victims . . ." (qtd. in Harrington
x).

Anonymous Work

When citing a work with no given author, use the first word of the title (excluding *a, an,* and *the*). In the following example the title referenced is *The
Local Theater Guide.*

Abingdon boasts The Barter Theater, one of the oldest playhouses in
the Commonwealth of Virginia (*Local* 1).

Electronic Sources

Electronic sources and documents provide either page numbers or paragraph numbers, and in many cases neither. When page numbers are
present, use the citation rules outlined above for texts. If the electronic
source uses paragraph numbers, use the abbreviation *par.* or *pars.,* and cite
the paragraph(s) referenced.

According to a review in the *Electronic Journal for Small Theaters*, Theater
South's new production of Marsha Norman's *'night Mother* "lacks the
emotional profundity to ever rise above mediocrity" (Wilson par. 3).

In cases where neither page numbers nor paragraph numbers are present, you can use the following abbreviations to indicate certain types of divisions within the source: "pt." for part; "sec." for section; "ch." for chapter; and "vol." for volume.

> In Middleton and Rowley's *A Fair Quarrel,* the surgeon's speeches in Acts 4 and 5 were borrowed from Peter Lowe's *A Discourse of the Whole Art of Chirurgery* (Hess sec. 2).

In situations where page or paragraph numbers are not provided and no divisions are present within the source, reference the source with a name only.

> Despite the evidence put forth to characterize Shylock as a Machiavellian villain, labeling him as such would be selling him short. It would be a simple reading of a complex character (Newton).

No page or paragraph numbers are needed when citing an electronic source in which the entries are alphabetically ordered (i.e., online encyclopedia).

> During the final stage of his writing career, Ibsen focused on symbolism. The plays *The Master Builder* (1892) and *John Gabriel Borkmann* (1896) "fused a contemplative realism with folk poetry" ("Ibsen, Henrik").

MLA "WORKS CITED" GUIDE

Examples compiled by Brian Barker.

Books

A Single Author
In referencing a book with one author, present the author's name (last name first), the title of the book (underlined or italicized), the city and publisher, and the date published.

Ball, David. *Backwards and Forwards: A Technical Manual for Reading Plays.* Carbondale, IL: Southern Illinois UP, 1983.

Two or Three Authors
In citing a book with two or three authors, only the lead author's name is reversed.

Mitchley, Jack, and Peter Spalding. *Five Thousand Years of Theatre*. New York: Holmes & Meier, 1982.

More Than Four Authors

When citing a book with four or more authors, the abbreviation et al. may be used.

Pickering, Thomas, et al. *Studying Drama: A Handbook.* London: Croom Helm, 1983.

Two or More Entries by the Same Author

Provide the author's full name in the first reference only. In the following citations, replace the name with three hyphens and a period.

Bentley, Eric. *The Life of the Drama.* New York: Athaeneum, 1964.
---. *The Theory of the Modern Stage: An Introduction to Modern Theatre and Drama.* New York: Penguin, 1968.

Collection Produced by an Editor(s)

Treat the names of editor(s) just as you would author(s). Use the abbreviation ed. to indicate the role of the editor.

Guernsey, Otis L., Jr., and Jeffrey Sweet, ed. *The Burns Mantle Theater Yearbook of 1989-1990.* New York: Applause, 1990.

Translated Work

For a translated book, provide the translator's name after the title.

Berthold, Margot. *The History of World Theater: From the Beginnings to the Baroque.* Trans. Edith Simmons. New York: Continuum, 1991.

Multivolume Work

In citing a multivolume work, provide the number of volumes in the collection after the title.

Young, William C. *Famous Actors and Actresses of the American Stage.* 2 vols. New York: R. R. Bowker Co., 1975.

Book in a Series

In citing a book that belongs to a series, provide the series name (no quotation marks or underline) and number after the book title. The series editor is not required.

Hewes, Henry, ed. *Famous American Plays of the 1940s.* The Laurel Drama Series, LXX119. New York: Dell, 1960.

Work with Subsequent Editions
If the work cited is a revised edition, reference the edition after the title.

Bordman, Gerald Martin. *The Oxford Companion to American Theatre.* 2nd ed. New York: Oxford UP, 1983.

Reprinted or Reissued Book
Indicate the original publication date of a reprinted book after the title.

Miller, Arthur. *After the Fall: A Play.* 1964. New York: Bantam, 1967.

A Work from an Anthology
When citing a work from an edited book or anthology, place the name of the author of the work first, followed by the title of the selection in quotation marks. Provide the title of the work (italicized or underlined) and the editor(s). Close the citation with the inclusive page numbers.

Stein, Roger B. "*The Glass Menagerie* Revisited: Catastrophe without Violence." *Tennessee Williams's The Glass Menagerie.* Ed. Harold Bloom. New York: Chelsea House, 1988. 7–20.

Citing an Introduction, Preface, Foreword, or Afterword
When citing an introductory or concluding work, give the author of that work first, followed by the type of piece (Preface, Afterword, etc.). After the book title, provide the name of the book's author. Close the citation with the inclusive page numbers of the referenced work.

Vidal, Gore. Introduction. *Collected Stories.* By Tennessee Williams. New York: New Directions Publishing Corporation, 1985. xix–xxv.
Esslin, Martin. Introduction. *The Encyclopedia of World Theater.* 4th ed. Ed. Esslin. New York: Scribner, 1977. 5–7.

Encyclopedia Articles (Signed and Unsigned)
In this citation, the citation does not require volume or page numbers. In citing encyclopedias, the publisher's name may be omitted, but the publication date must be included. If the author's name is available, place it first. If no author is given, place the title first.

Lahr, John. "Albee, Edward Franklin." *Colliers Encyclopedia,* 1992 ed.
"O'Neill, Eugene (Gladstone)." *The New Encyclopedia Britannica: Micropaedia.* 15th ed. 1995.

Other Reference Books
Provide complete publication information when citing articles from other types of reference books, especially those that are lesser known.

Adler, Jacob H. "Tennessee Williams." *Critical Survey of Drama*. Ed. Frank N. Magill. 7 vols. Pasadena, CA: Salem Press, 1994.

Unpublished Dissertation
The title of a dissertation is enclosed in quotation marks. Label it with the abbreviation *Diss.* and close with the university and year.

Nickel, Judith Sebesta. "A Spatial Analysis of Feminist Performance in the United States." Diss. University of Texas at Austin, 1997.

Indicating Unknown Publication Information
If certain publication information is unavailable, use the following abbreviations: n.p. for "no place of publication," n.p. for "no publisher given," and n.d. for "no date."

Doe, John. *The Invisible Shakespeare*. N.p.: n.p., n.d.

Articles in Periodicals

Article in a Scholarly Journal, Continuous Pagination
In a continuously paginated journal, the page numbers do not begin over with page 1 in a new issue; instead, pages run consecutively through all the issues in a volume. Following the author's name, provide the article title enclosed in quotation marks. The title of the journal comes next (underlined or italicized), followed by the volume number. Close the citation with the year (in parentheses) and the inclusive page numbers. In referencing a continuously paginated journal, you need not include the issue number or the month of publication.

Bowyer, T. H. "Warren Hastings in the Drama of Lion Feuchtwanger and Bertolt Brecht: Contexts and Connections." *Comparative Drama* 31 (1997): 394–414.

Article in a Scholarly Journal Paginated by Issue
For a journal paginated by issue, it is necessary to provide the issue number in the volume.

Schecner, Richard. "Drama, Script, Theatre, Performance." *The Drama Review* 17.3 (1973): 5–36.

Article in a Monthly Publication
For this type of periodical, provide the month and year of the issue. Do not include a volume or issue number.

Kowinski, William Severini. "The Play Looks Good on Paper—But Will It Fly?" *Smithsonian* Mar. 1992: 78–84.

Article in a Weekly Publication

In citing a weekly publication, provide the day, month, and year. Omit volume and issue numbers from your citation.

Brustein, Robert. "The Dreams of Ingmar Bergman." *New Republic* 29 July 1991: 29–31.

Newspaper Article

For a daily newspaper article, underline or italicize the title of the newspaper, omitting any initial articles (*a, an,* and *the*). Provide the complete date of publication (day, month, year). If the newspaper indicates an edition, provide it in your citation; articles often appear in different locations in separate editions. If given, include section letters before the page numbers. The second example illustrates how to present a particular edition and a section number.

Koehler, Robert. "A Methodical *Diary of a Madman.*" *Los Angeles Times* 12 Feb. 1993: F29.
Kerr, Walter. "When One Inspired Gesture Illuminates the Stage." *New York Times* 8 Jan. 1984, late ed., sec. 2: 1+.

Signed Editorial, Letter to the Editor, Review

Indicate the type of piece—Letter, Rev. of (for Review), Editorial—after the title. When citing a review, also provide the name of the reviewed piece with underline or quotation marks as appropriate.

Triplett, William. "A Bad *Word.*" Rev. of a performance of the play *They Never Said a Word,* by the Rose Organization at Theatre J. *Washington Post* 10 Jun. 1996: B3.
Ravage, Barbara. "Pricey Theater Preview." Letter. *New York Times* 27 Jan. 1998: A18.

Other Sources

Television and Radio

For television and radio entries, include the title of the episode or segment, title of program (underlined or italicized), network name, call letters and city of local station, broadcast date, and any other pertinent information.

"Lloyd Webber's *Sunset Boulevard* Opens on Broadway." *Showbiz Today.* CNN, New York. 18 Nov. 1994.
Middlemarch. By George Eliot. Adapt. Andrew Davies. Dir. Anthony Pope. Perf. Juliet Aubrey and Patrick Malahide. 6 episodes. Masterpiece Theatre. Intro. Russell Baker. PBS. WGBH, Boston. 10 Apr.–15 May 1994.
"Shakespearean Putdowns." Narr. Robert Siegel and Linda Wertheimer. *All Things Considered.* Natl. Public Radio. WNYC, New York. 6 Apr. 1994.

When the reference addresses the work of a specific person(s), place their name(s) in front of the title.

Lapine, James, dir. *Into the Woods*. By Stephen Sondheim. Perf. Bernadette Peters and Joanna Gleason. American Playhouse. PBS. WNET, New York. 3 Mar. 1991.

Film, Video, or Sound Recording
For film and video entries, include the medium and distributor. The citation may also include other pertinent information about the performers, director, producer, etc.

Death of a Salesman. By Arthur Miller. Dir. Volker Schlondorff. Perf. Dustin Hoffman, Charles Durning, Kate Reid, Stephen Lang, John Malkovich. Videocassette. Roxbury and Punch Production, 1986.

When the reference addresses the work of a specific person(s), place their name(s) in front of the title.

Shakespeare, William. *Othello*. Perf. Laurence Olivier, Maggie Smith, Frank Finlay, and Derek Jacobi. Dir. John Dexter. LP. RCA Victor, 1964.

Performance
For performance entries, include the title, author or composer, director, performers, theatre, city, date of the performance, and any other pertinent information.

Hamlet. By William Shakespeare. Dir. John Gielgud. Perf. Richard Burton. Shubert Theatre, Boston. 4 Mar. 1964.

When the reference addresses the work of a specific person or group, place their name(s) in front of the title.

Rigg, Diana, perf. *Medea*. By Euripides. Trans. Alistair Elliot. Dir. Jonathan Kent. Longacre Theatre, New York. 7 Apr. 1994.

Interview
Place the name of the person interviewed first. If the interview has a title, place it next in quotations. The word *Interview* can be used if no title is available; do not underline, italicize, or enclose it in quotations. If the interview is part of a larger work, include the title of the work in italics. Conclude with the interviewer's name (if significant) and other pertinent bibliographical information.

Norman, Marsha. Interview. *American Voices: Five Contemporary Playwrights in Essays and Interviews.* Interview with Esther Harriot. Jefferson, NC: McFarland, 1988. 148–163.

Wilson, August. Interview. *A Conversation with August Wilson.* Dir. Matteo Bellinelli. Videocassette. San Francisco, CA: California Newsreel, 1992.

For an interview that you conducted, provide the name of the person interviewed, the type of interview (personal, telephone, etc.), and the date.

Barker, Brian. Personal interview. 17 December 1997.

CD-ROMs

CD-ROMs with a Print Equivalent

Provide the author's name, print information (article in quotation marks, magazine or journal italicized or underlined, volume and page, date printed), the name of the database underlined or italicized, CD-ROM, the provider or vendor, and the publication date of the CD-ROM. Some of this information may not be available or may not be relevant to your reference.

CD-ROMs with No Print Equivalent

Provide the author's name, title of the article in quotation marks, article's original date, the name of the database underlined or italicized, CD-ROM, the provider or vendor, and the publication date of the CD-ROM. Some of this information may not be available or may not be relevant to your reference.

CD-ROM or Diskette as an Individual Publication

Provide the author's name, title (italicized or in quotation marks), product title (underlined), version/release information, CD-ROM *or* diskette, and publication information. Some of this information may not be available or may not be relevant to your reference.

Miller, Arthur. *The Crucible.* CD-ROM. New York: Penguin, 1994.

Online Sources: Computer Services

Online Sources with a Print Equivalent

Provide the author's name, print equivalent information (article title in quotation marks; title of publication underlined or italicized; original publication date), name of the database (underlined or italicized), Online, name of the computer service (AOL, Lexis, etc.), and the access date.

Bruckner, D. J. R. *"Song at Sunset*: Just about Everyone O'Casey Knew." *New York Times* 27 Jan. 1998: E3. *New York Times Online.* <http://www.nytimes.com/yr/mo/day/news/arts/> AOL. 28 Jan. 1998.

Online Sources with No Print Equivalent

Provide the author's name, article title in quotation marks, the date posted (if available), name of the database (underlined or italicized), Online, name of the computer service (AOL, Lexis, etc.), and the access date.

Evans, Greg. *"King and I* to End Broadway Run." 28 Jan. 1998. *AOL News.* Online. AOL. 30 Jan. 1998.

World Wide Web and Other Internet Sources

In citing online sources, provide the following information (when available): author's name; title of article in quotation marks; title of the journal, magazine, newsletter, conference, etc. (underlined or italicized); identifying numbers (volume number, issue number, etc.); date of electronic publication or of the latest update (in parentheses); page numbers or number of paragraphs (if none is provided, use the abbreviation *n. pag.* for no pagination); publication medium (*Online*); name of computer network (Internet, BITNET, etc.); date when you accessed the source; and electronic address or URL of the source.

World Wide Web, Article in a Reference Database

"Shaw, George Bernard." *Britannica Online.* Vers. 97.1.1 (Jan. 1998): n. pag. 6 Jan. 1998. Available <http://www.eb.com:180/cgi.bin/g?DocF=micro/541/46.html>

World Wide Web, Article in a Journal

Schneider, Ben Ross, Jr. *"King Lear* in Its Own Time: The Difference that Death Makes." *Early Modern Literary Studies* 1.1 (1995): 49 pars. 5 Jan. 1998. Available <http://purl.oclc.org/emls/01-1/schnlear.html>

World Wide Web, Article in a Magazine

Haun, Harry. "The Razzle-Dazzle of *Chicago's* Hinton Battle." *Playbill On-Line.* (21 Dec. 1997.): n. pag. 5 Jan. 1998. Available <http://www1.playbill.com/cgi.bin/plb/feature?cmd=show&code=+83692>

FTP (File Transfer Protocol) Sites

Diamond, Richard. "Seeing One's Way: The Image and Action of *Oidipous Tyrannos." Electronic Antiquity* 1.1 (1993): 5pp. 29 Jan. 1998. Available <FTP://ftp.utas.edu.au/departments/classics/antiquity/1%2C1-June1993/%284%29Articles/Diamond-Sophocles>

Gopher Sites

Snyder, Joel. "Seeing Theater with Your Ears." (Feb. 1995): n. pag. 26 Jan. 1998.
Available <http://gopher.tmn.com:70/0/Artswire/ad/article1.txt>

Ylinen, Topi. "Synopsis of the Plot of Wagner's *Ring.*" (29 Jan. 93): n. pag. 26 Jan.
1998. Available <gopher://wiretap.spies.com//00/Library/Music/Misc/
wagner.rng>

Synchronous Communications

Discussion List Posting

Merrian, Joanne. "Spinoff: Monsterpiece Theatre." *The Global Electronic Shakespeare
Conference* (30 Apr. 1994): n. pag. 27 Aug. 1997. Available <http://www.arts.
ubc.ca/english.iemls/shak/MONSTERP_SPINOFF.txt>

E-Mail

Critic, Joe. "The Play Is Worth Seeing." Personal e-mail. 26 Jan. 1998.

INDEX

Action, dramatic, 54–56 (diagram 56), 66
Analysis. *See* Text, analysis of
Aristotle, 11, 54–55, 92
Artaud, Antonin, 93
Audience, 19, 29–30
    for dramatic theory and the theatrical essay, 88–89, 95
    for reviews, 42–44
    for text analyses, 53
    for theater history, 72

Barish, Jonas, 93
Barker, Brian, 99, 105, 109
Barrymore, John, 20–22
Benchley, Robert, 19, 20, 22
Bentley, Eric, 97–98
Brecht, Bertolt, 92, 96–97

Catharsis, 11
CD-ROM documentation, 115
Childress, Alice, 90–91
Churchill, Caryl, 60–61
Citation of sources, 104–117
Clurman, Harold, 57
Collier, Jeremy, 93
Computers, 14, 81
Corrigan, Mary Ann, 11
Critical analysis, 15. *See also* Log; Writing, and learning

Critical thinking. *See* Writing, and learning
Criticism, 2. *See also* Reviews
    sources for, 101–103
Crothers, Rachel, 90–91

Dialogue
    in playtexts, 57–61
    writing (exercise), 16
Documentation. *See* Citation of sources
Drafting, 23, 26–31
    dummy, 25–26, 80
    rough, 27, 80
Drama, as distinguished from theatre, 1
Dramatic theory. *See* Theory

Editing, 36
    for grammar and usage, 36–38
    for punctuation, 37–38
    for spelling, 38–40
Essay, theatrical, 4–5, 88–98
    possible subjects for, 96

Feedback (for revision), 31, 33–36
Finley, Karen, 94
Flats, building of, 18
Formatting
    of drafts, 27–29
    experiments with, 17–22
    for functional analysis, 65
    for literary analysis, 65

Credits